AF600304

A POETRY OF THINGS

A Poetry of Things

The Material Lyric in Habsburg Spain

MARY E. BARNARD

UNIVERSITY OF TORONTO PRESS
Toronto Buffalo London

Toronto Buffalo London
utorontopress.com

ISBN 978-1-4875-0918-7 (cloth)
ISBN 978-1-4875-3986-3 (EPUB)
ISBN 978-1-4875-3985-6 (PDF)

Library and Archives Canada Cataloguing in Publication

Title: A poetry of things : the material lyric in Habsburg Spain / Mary E. Barnard.
Names: Barnard, Mary E., 1944– author.
Series: Toronto Iberic ; 64.
Description: Series statement: Toronto Iberic ; 64 | Includes bibliographical references and index.
Identifiers: Canadiana (print) 20210172983 | Canadiana (ebook) 20210173114 | ISBN 9781487509187 (cloth) | ISBN 9781487539856 (PDF) | ISBN 9781487539863 (EPUB)
Subjects: LCSH: Spanish poetry – Classical period, 1500–1700 – History and criticism. | LCSH: Material culture in literature. | LCSH: Quevedo, Francisco de, 1580–1645 – Criticism and interpretation. | LCSH: Góngora y Argote, Luis de, 1561–1627 – Criticism and interpretation. | LCSH: Arguijo, Juan de, 1567–1628 – Criticism and interpretation. | LCSH: Carvajal y Mendoza, Luisa de, 1566–1614 – Criticism and interpretation.
Classification: LCC PQ6184 .B37 2021 | DDC 861/.309–dc23

University of Toronto Press acknowledges the financial assistance to its publishing program of the Canada Council for the Arts and the Ontario Arts Council, an agency of the Government of Ontario.

Canada Council for the Arts | Conseil des Arts du Canada

Funded by the Government of Canada | Financé par le gouvernement du Canada | Canada

Contents

Acknowledgments

I would like to express my appreciation to those who have helped in the production of this book. I am grateful to my colleagues Anne J. Cruz, Miguel Martínez, Ricardo Padrón, and María Cristina Quintero, who heard parts of chapters at conferences of the Renaissance Society of America and the Society for Renaissance and Baroque Hispanic Poetry, and whose comments helped bring my ideas into sharper focus. I thank Steve Dolph and Victor Sierra Matute for inviting me to give the keynote address at their "Subjects and Objects" conference at the University of Pennsylvania. I would also like to thank the anonymous readers, whose comments and suggestions helped me rethink and refine my arguments.

I am grateful to the galleries and museums that provided illustrations and to the courtesy extended by Adele West at the Picture Library of Oxford's Ashmolean Museum; Florian Kugler at the Kunsthistorisches Museum, Vienna; Pilar Acosta at the Instituto Andaluz del Patrimonio Histórico on behalf of the Museo de Bellas Artes, Seville; and Britt Bowen of the Harvard Art Museums. I owe a special thanks to Suzanne Rancourt of the University of Toronto Press for her unfailing support of my research on the material culture of early modern Spain. I am grateful to Barbara Porter for her indispensable guidance and Angela Wingfield for her careful copyediting.

Illustrations

A POETRY OF THINGS

Introduction: The Material Scene

Make the objects look as if they want to be there.

Robert Bresson, *Notes on the Cinematograph*

On visiting the court of Philip III in Valladolid in 1603, Peter Paul Rubens (1572–1640) remarked on the "connoisseurship" of the Duke of Lerma, the king's *valido* (favorite), who had commissioned works of art and acquired entire private collections for the king's residences and for his own. "[The duke] is not without knowledge of fine things," writes Rubens, "through the particular pleasure and practice he has in seeing every day so many splendid works of Titian, of Raphael and others, which have astonished me, both by their quality and quantity, in the king's palace, in the Escorial, and elsewhere" (Baer 2008, 47–9). Lerma's knowledge of fine paintings and his "pleasure" and "practice" in viewing them daily by walking through the royal residences, especially at the royal palace where his own fourteen-room suite was filled with paintings, capture the visual seduction that the paintings exerted as they entered into the intimate life of the collector. The fascination and interaction with paintings and other objects as discursive entities is typical of the period, not only by collectors like Lerma but also by those who wrote about them in the Spain of Philip III (r. 1598–1621).

This book is about the ways in which cultural objects and material sites were used by poets who were writing in the years around 1600, a time of remarkable artistic and literary production. A generation of extraordinary painters – El Greco, Velázquez, and Juan Pantoja de la Cruz, among the best known – and writers, like Miguel de Cervantes and Lope de Vega, illustrate the range and vitality of that moment at the turn of the century. I have selected the works of four poets who were fully part of that cultural efflorescence to illustrate the variety and originality of their highly personal experiments in what I call the "baroque material lyric."

Francisco de Quevedo (1580–1645), Luis de Góngora (1561–1627), Juan de Arguijo (1567–1623), and Luisa de Carvajal y Mendoza (1566–1614) were heirs of Garcilaso de la Vega (c. 1501–36), soldier and court poet who transformed Spanish letters by introducing Italianate verse forms, practices of imitation, an imperial subject, and a vibrant material lyric in which objects served as sites of discourse and cultural exchange (Barnard 2014). I explore how these poets continued Garcilaso's excursions into material culture, with special attention to the agency of objects. As if observing Robert Bresson's memorable dictum for cinematographers, they "make the objects look as if they want to be there." Performing within prescribed spaces, objects become interactive participants in the lyric enterprise to create, in effect, a rhetoric of the object in verse. If some objects have voice and "speak," others do not, but all engage in dialogic exchange with viewers and readers in a variety of venues across time and space. Books carry the "voices" of ancient authors to a solitary reader, and tombs "speak" to passersby on behalf of the entombed, while sculptures of Christ take on life to address a female mystic, antique statuary exhibited in a museum invite an exchange with a learned visitor, and ceiling paintings animate the meeting of an academy of humanists. It is that performative aspect of objects, whether they remain in situ or are gathered in a library, museum, or convent, that I find most compelling in the lyric I examine here.

Rubens intimated that Lerma's "practice" of viewing exhibited paintings, of routinely revisiting them, transformed the royal rooms into a space of visual pleasure, an act that exemplifies a theoretical notion pertinent to this study. It is what Michel de Certeau has termed a "practiced place," a dynamic, mobile space (*espace*) created by everyday activities, such as rituals and pilgrimages, in short, a specific physical location (*lieu*) activated and transformed by "walkers" ([1980] 1988, 117–18). Henri Lefebvre's triadic formulation of space as a social construct complements de Certeau. Particularly relevant here are what Lefebvre calls "perceived space" or "spatial practice," the daily routines and activities generated by society, and "lived space," what is produced by social interaction and cultural practices. Mediated through "images and symbols," it is the space of "inhabitants" and "users" that "the imagination seeks to change and appropriate" ([1974] 1991, 38–9).[1] The notion of space as socially and culturally produced is highly suggestive for my incursions into the world of objects and material sites, and the questions they raise about memory and history, vision and voice, the formation of identity, and the construction of texts.

That sense of space, in which a human presence endows a material place with movement and cultural meaning, is illustrated by an anecdote involving physicists Niels Bohr and Werner Heisenberg during their visit to Kronberg Castle in Denmark. Bohr says to Heisenberg:

> Isn't it strange how this castle changes as soon as one imagines that Hamlet lived here? As scientists we believe that a castle consists only of stones, and admire the way the architect put them together. The stones, the green roof with its patina, the wood carvings in the church, constitute the whole castle. None of this should be changed by the fact that Hamlet lived here, and yet it is changed completely. Suddenly the walls and the ramparts *speak* a quite different language. The courtyard becomes an entire world, a dark corner reminds us of the darkness in the human soul, we hear Hamlet's "To be or not to be." Yet all we really know about Hamlet is that his name appears in a thirteenth-century chronicle. No one can prove that he really lived, let alone that he lived here. But everyone knows the questions Shakespeare had him ask, the human depths he was made to reveal, and so he, too, had to be found a place on earth, here in Kronberg. And once we know that, Kronberg becomes quite a different castle for us. (Heisenberg 1972, 51; my emphasis)

Yi-Fu Tuan, who in *Space and Place: The Perspective of Experience* (1977) cites this passage, asks, "What is a place? What gives a place its identity, its aura?," then adds, "How can a mere legend haunt Kronberg Castle and impart a mood that infiltrates the minds of two famous scientists?" (4–5). Tuan's questions, relating the scientists' reaction to the self-contained world of the castle, are prompted by his interest in the subjective and the affective as tools for his understanding of place and space.[2] The spatial theories of de Certeau and Lefebvre offer ways of answering his question from a layered perspective. The scientists, the "walkers" who bring their cultural knowledge to bear on Kronberg by recalling the words of Shakespeare's Hamlet, animate and transform the castle – the stones, the roof with its patina, the wood carvings that "speak" his language – into a dark space of melancholy. Reminiscing on what they have read, the scientists "feel" the prince's aura, his darkness emanating from the castle's architecture.

That paradigm of visitors producing a space by projecting a cultural memory on a material site appears in several guises in the poems I analyse here. A pilgrim visiting Rome reads the artefacts preserved in the Capitoline Museum through his humanist learning. Passers-by "hear" the voices of a wood fragment and a marble slab "speaking" through lapidary inscriptions in the tradition of ancient tomb poems. Humanists meeting in an academy interpret a mythological ceiling painting through ancient texts; a mystic engages with statues of Christ through textual and visual knowledge, and spiritual practices; and a reworking of the myth of Polyphemus and Galatea is mapped within a set of interactive landscapes filled with artefacts, where actors, "walkers," enter to stage their performances. In each case it is the interplay of place, object, text, and memory that produces a distinctive cultural space.

The Spain of Philip III

The material lyric studied here was a lyric of its time, when the powerful and wealthy acquired and prominently displayed fine objects of ancient and recent provenance. Philip II (r. 1556–98) had amassed thousands of relics, religious art, jewellery, and books, as well as paintings, both religious and secular, commissioned from the most accomplished artists, including Tintoretto, Veronese, and especially Titian (Sánchez Cantón 1956–9). Philip III's extravagant wedding to Margaret of Austria in 1599 set the tone for a new era of collecting and flaunting fine objects.[3] His entourage included writers, patrons, and artists, notably Lope de Vega and his patron the marquis of Sarría, known as the Count of Lemos, to whom Cervantes would dedicate part 2 of the *Quixote* (1615), and Juan Pantoja de la Cruz, the official court portrait painter, who portrayed the young king, only twenty years old at his accession, as a powerful monarch dressed in armour, embodying opulence and magnificence, the "new style of grandeur" for the king's public persona (fig. 0.1).[4] The manipulation of visual imagery to shape a viewer's perception was not new at court. Philip III's ancestors, Emperor Maximilian I (r. 1508–19) and his grandson Charles V (Holy Roman Emperor, r. 1519–56; king of Spain, 1516–56), commissioned works of art from the best craftsmen and artists of their time – notably Albrecht Dürer for Maximilian, Titian for Charles – to "market" themselves.[5] They understood how reception involved an exchange between the portrait's image and the viewer's understanding of royal majesty.

Like his predecessors, Philip III admired fine objects, but it was Francisco Gómez de Sandoval, the Duke of Lerma and the king's favourite (1598–1618), who was the true patron of the arts and who played a major role in the formation of baroque art culture in Spain. Lerma's sense of entitlement led to his commissioning Rubens to paint his portrait, a magnificent equestrian painting that recalls Titian's equestrian portrait *Charles V at Mühlberg* and more significantly the equestrian statue of

Figure 0.1 Juan Pantoja de la Cruz, *King Philip III of Spain*, 1601–4. Kunsthistorisches Museum, Vienna. KHM-Museumsverband.

Figure 0.2 Peter Paul Rubens, *Equestrian Statue of the Duke of Lerma*, 1603. Museo del Prado, Madrid. © Museo Nacional del Prado / Art Resource, New York.

Marcus Aurelius in Rome's Capitoline Museum (fig. 2.5).[6] As a prolific collector in his own right, with an array of tapestries, jewels, reliquaries, and almost nine hundred pieces of glass and ceramics displayed in a special *camarín* in his palace in Madrid, Lerma set an example for wealthy and well-placed aristocrats for collecting antiquities as well as finely crafted objects, as was the custom in Italy. The frenzied quest for antiquities in Rome led Francisco de Quevedo, walking among the ruins of the city in 1617, to lament that the impulse to collect had led the *curiosos* to pilfer fragments of once "living" ancient statuary, which he admired and dialogued with at the Capitoline – in particular the statue of Marcus Aurelius.

The cultural life of Spain under Philip III was continually enriched by artistic and literary developments both at home and from beyond the peninsula. Quevedo dialogued with ancient Roman and Greek writers and contemporary vernacular and neo-Latin poets, Carvajal absorbed Christian hagiography and mystical writings, while Arguijo and Góngora reconceived ancient myth. Foreign artists, especially from the Netherlands and Italy, were invited to work in Spain. Italy exercised an especially strong attraction: visitors marvelled at the sites in Rome, and the wealthy imported antiquities for display in their residences and gardens as signifiers of refined taste. Private academies founded under the influence of Castiglione's *Il Cortegiano* and based on Italian models provided occasions beyond educational settings for open discussion of classical and contemporary texts and for the formation of social networks. One of the earliest academies, founded in Seville by scholar and poet Juan de Mal Lara, was continued by Francisco Pacheco, a distinguished painter and author of the famous treatise *El arte de la pintura,* who took in a young Velázquez as his apprentice in 1611 (Brown 1978, 21). Pacheco inspired Arguijo and the Duke of Alcalá to establish their own academies in Seville.[7]

Beyond the court and private palaces of the nobles and the wealthy, the most powerful force in Spanish society during the Counter-Reformation was the Church. Religious orders, especially the Jesuits, exerted an enormous influence on daily life, enforcing the canons of the Council of Trent (1563) and embedding a strident religiosity within the very fabric of Spanish life. Yet religious communities also were major patrons of artists, commissioning liturgical objects, paintings, and sculptures for their cathedrals, monasteries, and parish churches, thereby contributing to the profusion of fine objects visible in public spaces (Schroth 2008, 95–118). Collections, whether of secular or religious art, also had a role in private spaces as "frames for spiritual retreat" (marco de retiro espiritual) away from the court and the "world," following a spiritual and moral calling, as Miguel Morán and Fernando Checa have observed (1985, 194). Charles V served as model when he took favourite paintings, Titian's *Ecce Homo* among others, from his collection to the monastery of Yuste when he retired in 1556. Don Diego de Vich, the keeper of Philip III's jewels (guardajoyas), retired to a Valencia monastery, where he lived surrounded by his paintings, as did the Seville notables we will encounter in this study, Francisco de Medina and Rodrigo Caro.

The commerce in fine objects, the extravagance of the court, and the power of the monarchy and the Church accompanied other powerful currents in the Spain of Philip III. War was always in the air, with Spanish forces involved in conflicts with major European states. The Pax Hispanica instituted by Philip to end the wars of religion was implemented only gradually (the Peace of Vervis with France in 1598; the Treaty of London in 1604; and the truce with the Spanish Netherlands in 1609).[8] Despite "the power of the monarchy and the richness of its court culture," writes Antonio Feros, "Spaniards were also aware that they were living in what Don Quijote called an Age of Iron, when economic crisis was creating an enormous army of vagabonds and criminals, when war was destroying the financial and moral foundations of the society, a time defined by anxieties, plagues, political corruption, military defeats, violence, and religious persecution" (2008, 16). Political discord exacerbated those tensions: Lerma was removed from office in 1618, and some of his men were imprisoned – Alonso Ramírez de Prado and Pedro Franqueza in 1607 – and Rodrigo Calderón, Count of Oliva, was arrested and executed in 1621 (Feros 2000). There was no agreement as to the true origins of the country's current state (political, social, or moral), but it was clear that Spain was in crisis.[9] The picaresque novel– whether produced anonymously like *Lazarillo de Tormes* (published in 1554 but still in vogue) or by luminaries like Francisco de Quevedo in *La vida del Buscón* (written around 1604) and Miguel de Cervantes in *Rinconete y Cortadillo* (1613) – reflected the social ills of the times (Cruz 1999). Quevedo's focus on ruins exemplifies the feeling of political and social decline. Luisa de Carvajal y Mendoza makes the Madrid of the poor and vagabonds a stage for her Franciscan virtues of poverty and humility in a kind of exhibitionistic performance to confront and upstage her aristocratic family and friends.

Four Poets

I have selected poems that best illustrate the treatment of objects and material sites in four poets of markedly different lives and aesthetic temperament. Francisco de Quevedo had the closest ties to the royal court, where he was educated. The most important position of his father, Pedro Gómez de Quevedo, at court was as secretary to Queen Anne, daughter of María of Austria and Holy Roman Emperor Maximilian II; his mother, María de Santibáñez, was lady-in-waiting to Queen Anne – the fourth and last wife of Philip II – who died in 1580, the year Quevedo was born. He had powerful enemies but also powerful friends, like the Duke of Osuna, who figures prominently in this study.[10] A prolific writer of both poetry and prose and an abundant correspondence, Quevedo was drawn to objects that served as carriers of culture and as epistemological sites of discourse.

Chapter 1 ("The Agency of Objects") examines several examples of his "conversations" with the past through objects. "Voices" of the dead, awakened through the reading of books, actively engage a reader who "listens" to them with his eyes and whose own writing is thereby enriched. Voices emanating from the tombs of Christopher Columbus and the Duke of Osuna call out to passers-by in the tradition of ancient tomb poems, illustrating Paul de Man's concept of ekphrasis as a "speaking out," of giving voice to a silent image or object (1984). The passers-by create a "practiced place," in Michel de Certeau's formulation, and a social memory of the tomb and its occupant. Quevedo's apostrophe to the paintbrush celebrates an instrument that retrieves the past, not through voice but through image. Whether in its portraits of the dead who have "fled memory," in a miniature of an absent beloved, or in Egyptian hieroglyphs encoded with visual memory, the paintbrush initiates exchanges between the painted object and the viewer across cultural, historical, and political boundaries. Quevedo's poems are striking examples of Roger Chartier's observation in *Inscription and Erasure* (2007) that memory resides on a material substrate, whether a printed page, an incised marble tomb, or a painted canvas.

Chapter 2 ("Material Rome") follows Quevedo's walk through Rome, which inspired his *silva* "Roma antigua y moderna," an extended meditation on Roman civilization, its collapse, and the transformation of Rome into a papal city. In seeking to capture the essence of ancient Rome through his wandering, he practises what the cultural geographer Carl Sauer calls the "morphology of landscape," relating the physical landscape to its cultural impress ([1925] 1967). For Quevedo the pilgrim, the city's ancient bridges, triumphal arches, and temples in ruin, and the "rescued" statuary in the Capitoline Museum, evoke a complex cultural memory. Relying on the ancient notion that places and monuments serve as repositories of memory, as in Livy's *History of Rome* and Virgil's *Aeneid*, he finds imperial Rome not in its now-decayed built environment but in its salvaged artefacts, especially the equestrian statue of Marcus Aurelius. Quevedo's reading of imperial Rome and its surviving objects, through textual fragments adapted from the ancients and from early modern poems of ruins, especially those of Joachim du Bellay and Janus Vitalis, gives the *silva* its distinctive quality. Yet the *silva* ultimately is not a traditional poem of ruins, for it ends by celebrating the reborn, hybrid Rome of the humanist popes, who preserved the city's material remains and became guardians of its past.

Chapter 3 ("Producing Pastoral Spaces") analyses Luis de Góngora's *Fábula de Polifemo y Galatea*. Born in Córdoba, Góngora studied at the University of Salamanca, took minor orders, and followed his uncle as prebendary of the cathedral chapter in Córdoba. Ordained a priest in 1605, he served briefly as chaplain to Philip III.[11] As the supreme exponent of *culteranismo*, his *Polifemo*, a recasting of the Ovidian myth of Polyphemus and Galatea, is the most refined poem of the baroque material lyric. I read the *Polifemo* as a set of landscapes replete with objects, where even time and sonority are materialized. My reading is inspired by the distinction drawn by de Certeau between a stable, physical place and the social activity that transforms it into a "practiced place," and by W.J.T. Mitchell's framing of landscape as "a natural scene mediated by culture" ([1994] 2002, 5), which stresses the role of visual interaction in the construction of identity, in particular between the lovers Galatea and Acis in a *locus amoenus* fraught with tense visual encounters. Each space contains appropriate objects – trappings of the hunt for the count, handmade tools for the shepherd Polyphemus, and refined gifts for Galatea. The poem is difficult and complex, a powerful baroque narrative of wit and artifice.

Chapter 4 ("Staging Myth") probes the original experiment of Juan de Arguijo, a wealthy patron of the arts in Seville, who wrote two sonnets as commentaries on the mythological panels painted on the ceiling of his library in 1601 for viewing by his academy of humanist friends.[12] Inspired by the painted ceilings in GiorgioVasari's house in Arezzo, Arguijo's ceiling became in turn a model for the Duke of Alcalá, whose ceiling in his palace, the Casa de Pilatos, painted in 1603 by Francisco Pacheco, survives today with Arguijo's as rare examples of ceiling paintings in Spain. Two years before Rubens marvelled at Lerma's "practice" of viewing the royal art collection, Arguijo's academy had engaged his scenes of Phaëton, who ignores his father's admonitions not to fly too close to the sun, and of Ganymede, who surrendered to Jupiter in a homoerotic encounter. In casting ancient myths in paintings, interpreted by poems that speak for them, and staging the two interrelated media for viewing and commentary by the humanists of the academy who met in his library, Arguijo created an entirely novel form of the material lyric. To understand the critical role played by his academy, I adopt Jerome McGann's observation that texts are produced and reproduced under specific social and institutional conditions, and that every text is a social event "where certain communicative interchanges are being practiced" (1991, 21) That interplay between text, the material, and social context transformed Arguijo's library into a staged event for the creation of collective memory.

Chapter 5 ("A Mystic and Her Objects") examines the poems of Luisa de Carvajal y Mendoza, who was influenced as much by her material surroundings as by the tradition of Catholic spirituality. I privilege the intimate relation between interiority and materiality, epistemology and vision, and writing and memory. Her texts are suffused with the material culture of her times, including the artefacts that surrounded her aristocratic upbringing at court – tapestries, precious stones, and fancy clothing – as well as the religious paintings and sculptures of the Royal Alcázar and the Monasterio de las Descalzas Reales, a convent of noble born Franciscan nuns, which she frequently visited when living next to Juana de Austria's palace.[13] Powerfully drawn to the images of Christ's body, especially to his wounds at the column of flagellation, she imagines herself entering his body in mystical union and placing her tomb within it, while Christ, materially present, speaks out from the marble sculpture and inscribes her tomb with an epitaph. Yet Carvajal could not escape the material world of her upbringing. While leading a highly public life as an impoverished missionary in Jacobean London, she sought scissors and spindles for spinning gold thread for sale at market in order to support herself and her companions. Whether in her mystical poetry or her work with the poor, Carvajal ultimately was unable to overcome the material culture of the aristocratic world of the court and her family, the Carvajal and Mendoza clans.

The objects in *A Poetry of Things* – books, tombstones, a paintbrush, urban ruins, antique statuary, musical instruments, ceiling paintings, portraits, miniatures, and religious statuary – served as vehicles for exploring issues of moment in Philip III's Spain: the preservation of humanist learning in the age of print; the collapse of empires, specifically of imperial Rome and implicitly of Habsburg Spain; the role of learned academies in the literary and artistic life beyond the court; the formation of subjective identities within distinct social spaces; and the role of religious objects in the tradition of spirituality of Counter-Reformation Spain. My readings have been enriched by new ways of understanding the agency of objects in lyric discourse and by the key role played by dialogic exchange in making the poems occasions for dynamic encounters between subjects and material objects.[14]

Chapter One

The Agency of Objects

Among Francisco de Quevedo's elegant poems are memorable exemplars of the material lyric in which objects are endowed with agency to stage interactive performances with readers and viewers for mediating cultural and historical memory. The four texts examined in this chapter illustrate how books, tombs, and a paintbrush participate in that vibrant dialogic exchange. In the sonnet "Desde la Torre," books voice the learning of the ancients to a solitary reader, who listens to them with "his eyes," absorbing their wisdom. In the sonnet epitaphs to Christopher Columbus and the Duke of Osuna, a piece of wood and a marble slab speak the deeds of the entombed to passers-by in words set in inscriptions on their tombs. And in the *silva* "Al pincel," a paintbrush empowers paintings, a portrait miniature, and hieroglyphs encoded with visual memory to enact lively exchanges across cultural, historical, and political boundaries.[1] Quevedo's collection of discursive artefacts – printed, inscribed, and painted – could have been displayed in a Wunderkammer, where randomly acquired objects were valued as much for the "conversations" they initiated as for their aesthetic qualities.

In his *Inscription and Erasure,* Roger Chartier captures a fundamental aspect of the early modern quest to preserve memory through inscription on material surfaces. "Stone, wood, fabric, parchment, and paper all served as substrates on which the memory of events and men could be inscribed. In the open space of the city or the seclusion of the library, in majesty in books or in humility on more ordinary objects, the mission of the written was to dispel the obsession with loss" (2007, vii). If Chartier posits material substrates as mute carriers of script, of text, Quevedo ascribes voice to objects, which speak or speak out, as material interlocutors. For Chartier the issue is inscription and its erasure, "the durable record and the ephemeral text." For Quevedo, who also is sensitive to the threat of erasure, it is the dynamic created by the agency of objects that preserves memory through performance.

A Museum of Books

In his biography of Quevedo ([1663] 1988), Pablo de Tarsia writes that the poet was a voracious reader, always carrying with him "a museum" of books:

> Llevaba un Museo portátil de más de cien tomos de libros de letra menuda, que cabían todos en unas bisaças, procurando en el camino, y en las paradas lograr el tiempo con la lectura de los más curiosos y apacibles. Fue tan aficionado a libros, que apenas salía alguno, cuando le compraba. (Tarsia [1663] 1988, 34–5)
>
> (He carried with him a portable museum of more than a hundred books of tiny print fitted in leather bags, making sure on the road and wherever he stopped to find time to read the most unusual and enjoyable. He was so fond of books that as soon as one was published, he would buy it.)

"Museo" alerts us to the materiality of Quevedo's private collection of "curiosos" that he carried in leather bags as a kind of portable cabinet of curiosities,[2] objects that provided him with what Stephen Greenblatt calls the "resonance" of a museum experience: "the power of the displayed object to reach out beyond its formal boundaries to a larger world, to evoke in the viewer the complex, dynamic cultural forces from which it has emerged and for which it may be taken by a viewer to stand" (1991, 42). Greenblatt argues that behind the liturgical artefacts in the State Jewish Museum in Prague – ark curtains, Torah crowns, finials, pointers – lies the "act that mattered: not viewing but reading," a reading "bound up" with resonance (47). He explains: "this resonance depends not upon visual stimulation but upon a felt intensity of names, and behind the names, as the very term *resonance* suggests, of voices: the voices of those who chanted, studied, muttered their prayers, wept, and then were forever silenced" (47; italics in a original). Greenblatt's viewer "reads" voices in the artefacts. Quevedo's books, his personal collection of discursive artefacts, yield a resonance of their own, with voices of the dead awakened orally, aurally, and visually through his intimate act of reading in his country retreat in la Torre de Juan Abad.

In his sonnet "Desde la Torre" a meditation on reading in the silence of his retreat in southern La Mancha, books serve as epistemological sites for accessing the learning of the ancients through their "voices":[3]

Retirado en la paz de estos desiertos,
con pocos, pero doctos, libros juntos,
vivo en conversación con los difuntos
y escucho con mis ojos a los muertos.
Si no siempre entendidos, siempre abiertos,
o enmiendan, o fecundan mis asuntos;
y en músicos callados contrapuntos
al sueño de la vida hablan despiertos.
Las grandes almas que la muerte ausenta,
de injurias de los años, vengadora,
libra, ¡oh gran don Iosef!, docta la emprenta.
En fuga irrevocable huye la hora;
pero aquélla el mejor cálculo cuenta
que en la lección y estudios nos mejora. (1:253–4)

(Withdrawn to the peace of these solitary places
with a few but learned books,
I live in conversation with the dead,
listening to them with my eyes.
Always open, if not always understood,
they amend, they enrich my affairs
and in silent musical counterpoints
awake, they speak to the dream of life.
Oh Don Josef, for those great souls
taken by death, the learned
press avenges time's slanders.
In irrevocable flight the hour flees;
but it can be counted fortunate
when we better ourselves by reading.)

The oral component brought into lines 3–4 may have been inspired by one of Seneca's *Moral Epistles*, as James Crosby has noted (1994, 179). An aging Seneca writes to his friend Lucilius: "Most of my conversations are with books" ([1917–25] 2014, 2:67).[4] Quevedo might have recalled as well Seneca's other confession to his friend: "Whenever your letters arrive, I imagine that I am with you, and I have the feeling that I am about *to speak* my answer, *instead of writing it*. Therefore let us together investigate the nature of this problem of yours, just as if we were *conversing with one another*" (2:67; my emphasis).[5] Like Seneca, Quevedo shifts attention from the written page to an imagined orality, an act of speaking, but in the poet's case there is also a shift to an imagined aurality: reading books is conceived as a "visual hearing," allowing for his own conversation with dead authors. This silent performance is strengthened by a dialogic interaction structured through counterpoint: "en músicos callados contrapuntos / al sueño de la vida hablan despiertos" (in silent musical counterpoints, / awake, they speak to the dream of life). Polyphonic technique, with its weaving together of several melodic lines to create harmonies, establishes an intimate rapport between the lyric subject, the reader within the text, and the voices silently awakened through his reading. Speaking in counterpoint – *punctus contra punctum*, "point against point" or "note against note" – the textual voices establish a harmonious concord with the reader who is listening, mimicking the perfect conjoining of chords to create musical harmonies. Living in the golden age of vocal polyphony, Quevedo was well acquainted with choral music in Spain and in Italy, where he travelled as the secretary and confidant to Pedro Téllez Girón, the third duke of Osuna. He surely was familiar with the works of Tomás Luis de Victoria (c. 1548–1611), known as the Spanish Palestrina, the most famous composer of choral music in Quevedo's time. It is precisely his conversations with ancient authors that "amend" and "enrich" his own "affairs," that is, his literary production ("o enmiendan, o fecundan mis asuntos").

In retreating from the *negotium* of public life to his peaceful retreat, Quevedo had eminent predecessors. Petrarch revived the ancient notion of the contemplative life of *otium* that made possible artistic and philosophical creativity. Withdrawing from the activity of the papal court, he chose to live in a modest *villetta* in the Vaucluse near "a grotto with the source of the Sorgue," where he wrote the *Solitary Life* and his poems to Laura.[6] Marsilio Ficino found sanctuary in a *villetta* at Careggi (1462), a gift from his patron Cosimo de' Medici and a refuge that came to be known as the Platonic Academy, where he soothed his melancholy while living close to nature, pursuing his studies of Plato in quiet contemplation. Closer to Quevedo is Michel de Montaigne, who in 1571 withdrew from the *parlement* of Bordeaux to his estate in the Dordogne, where in his tower library of more than fifteen hundred volumes of classical, Italian, and French literature, philosophy, and history, he began to work on his *Essais*, first published in 1580 (Regosin 1995, 249). But Quevedo's retreat was not entirely solitary, animated as it was by a community of voices speaking through books.

Quevedo calls his books "doctos," denoting their origin in the classical learning that inspired the high culture of early modern Spain, the *poesía culta* to which his sonnet and a great portion of his literary corpus belong. In his biography Tarsia attests to this simple fact that for Quevedo books were "libros doctos": "Del amor de las letras se le engendró una muy particular estimación de los hombres doctos" (His love of letters engendered in him a particular esteem for learned men). But "learned" also qualifies the printing press, to which Quevedo renders homage as the instrument that makes possible the discursive field of his library. He assigns to that great technological invention for the communication of knowledge the mission to avenge the "great souls" that "death removes" – the very voices that he hears in his reading – by delivering them from the ravages of time: "Las grandes almas que la muerte ausenta, / de injurias de los años, vengadora, / libra, ¡oh gran don Iosef!, docta la emprenta."

The sonnet illustrates what D.F. McKenzie has called "the book as an expressive form," best understood not as a passive object but as a product of a complex production and continuing textual engagement ([1986] 1999, 1). McKenzie argued for a "sociology of texts" that accounts for their transmission and reception, as well as their interpretation (4). Chartier signalled the importance of that insight, of linking the analysis of symbolic meanings with the material form by which they are transmitted (2007, vii). Quevedo's discursive performance within the confines of his retreat demonstrates the full force of the ancient voices preserved in books, through which they are transmitted for his intellectual and moral profit ("que en la lección y estudios nos mejora"). Delighting in his material interlocutors and his access to the past, he carried his portable "museum" of books in order to maintain a constant conversation with the "great souls" who nourished his own writing ("fecundan mis asuntos"). Mindful of the role of his learned objects in enabling his conversations with the dead, Quevedo addresses his friend and editor, Josef Antonio González de Salas, celebrating him in the very naming, as the one who will make possible the transmission and preservation of the poet's own voice by publishing, posthumously in 1648, the first printed edition of his poems.

Speaking Tombs

Quevedo extended his conversations project to the burial ground where tomb inscriptions speak for the dead. In two notable sonnet epitaphs, voice is ascribed to funerary artefacts, a fragment of Christopher Columbus's ship buried with the admiral, and the marble of the Duke of Osuna's tomb. Their voices, addressing passers-by, call attention to themselves as material presences that take on life and assume agency in the tradition of ancient tomb poems: the wood fragment celebrates itself and Columbus, while the marble slab celebrates a great warrior who died in prison. By speaking out, Quevedo's ekphrastic tombs invite passers-by to a conversation on memory and history.

The Greek Anthology – a compendium of epigrams, songs, poems, epitaphs, and rhetorical exercises from the Classical through the Byzantine period – provided Quevedo with models for his sonnet epitaphs in epigrams memorializing the dead on imaginary tombstones, often addressed to an anonymous visitor or stranger, as in Tullius Laureas's epitaph for Sappho's tomb.[7] It reads: "When you pass, O Stranger, by the Aeolian tomb, say not that I, the Lesbian poet, am dead. This tomb was built by the hands of men, and such works of mortals are lost in swift oblivion. But if you enquire about me for the sake of the Muses, from each of whom I took a flower to lay beside my nine flowers of song, you shall find that I escaped the darkness of death, and that no sun shall dawn and set without memory of lyric Sappho" (*The Greek Anthology* 1970, 2:7.17). A stranger reading the inscription engages in an established cultural practice. Aristocratic families of Attica buried their dead in private burial grounds along the roadside of their estates or near Athens, with graves marked by relief sculpture, statues, and stelai inscribed with epitaphs, often in verse. The Romans continued the tradition of burying their dead in roadside tombs outside urban centres. "These memorials would have been seen and visited by many, and it was the visitor to the tombs – either family and friends or complete strangers – who kept the memory of the dead alive" (Carroll 2006, 1). Propertius referred to tombs as busy spots "where the crowd travels along an unsleeping thoroughfare" (2006, 3.16.25–6). "In a symbolic sense," writes Alain Gowing, "in order to arrive in Rome's present – in the city of the living – one was first required to travel through Rome's past, through a virtual community of the dead which was at once sacred, immutable, and unmovable" (2005, 13).

Within the fiction of Sappho's epigram, her voice summons a passer-by to hear her most intimate thoughts on memory and poetry. Her words are revealed through ekphrasis – understood here in its etymological sense of "a speaking out," giving voice to a silent image or object – *ek* "out," *phrasis* "to speak" (*Oxford English Dictionary*). Ekphrasis connects with the rhetorical trope of prosopopoeia, which in Paul de Man's inspired definition is a "fiction of an apostrophe to an absent, deceased, or voiceless entity, which posits the possibility of the latter's reply and confers upon it the power of speech. Voice assumes mouth, eye, and finally face, a chain manifest in the etymology of the trope's name, *prosopon poien*, to confer a mask or a face (*prosopon*)"

(1984, 75–6). Yet in the Sappho epigram it is not the one who apostrophizes, but instead the one who is customarily apostrophized who initiates the speaking out from the tomb. Sappho confers upon herself both the apostrophe and the power of speech of which de Man writes; an absent and voiceless Sappho assumes her mask to stage an act of self-remembrance, to remind the living that her "song" will survive beyond the grave.

Columbus and His Shipmate

In "Túmulo a Colón" (Tomb to Columbus) a personified piece of wood buried with Columbus confers upon itself the power of speech. Like Sappho, it assumes a mask to stage a performance to claim its own place in history and memory:

> Túmulo a Colón
> Habla un pedazo de la nave en que descubrió el nuevo mundo[8]
> Imperio tuve un tiempo, pasajero,
> sobre las ondas de la mar salada;
> del viento fui movida y respetada
> y senda abrí al Antártico hemisfero.
> Soy con larga vejez tosco madero;
> fui haya, y de mis hojas adornada,
> del mismo que alas hice en mi jornada,
> lenguas para cantar hice primero.
> Acompaño esta tumba tristemente,
> y aunque son de Colón estos despojos,
> su nombre callo, venerable y santo,
> de miedo que, de lástima, la gente
> tanta agua ha de verter con tiernos ojos,
> que al mar nos vuelva a entrambos con el llanto. (1:460)
>
> (Tomb to Columbus
> A piece of the ship in which he discovered the new world speaks
> An empire I had long ago, passer-by,
> on the waves of the salty sea;
> revered by the blowing winds,
> I paved a path to the Antarctic hemisphere.
> I am wood coarsened by years;
> once a beech, adorned by leaves,
> from it I made wings for sailing,
> but first I made tongues to sing.

Mournfully, I accompany this tomb,
and though Columbus's remains
lie here, his given name, holy and venerable,
I will not say, fearing that out of pity,
tender eyes will shed so much water
that we both will be washed out to sea again.)

The wood's voice, inscribed on the lapidary surface, calls out to the passer-by, who by listening becomes complicit in the act of remembrance: "Imperio tuve un tiempo, pasajero" (An empire I had long ago, passer-by). The *Diario de abordo,* an account of Columbus's first voyage, transcribed by Bartolomé de las Casas, relates an anecdote that explains how the piece of wood, a synecdoche for the ship, "died" toward the end of that voyage. On the night of 25 December 1492 Columbus's ship, the *nao* (carrack) *Santa María,* was grounded by the currents on a sand bar off the coast of Hispaniola. Columbus blames the master owner of the ship ("maestre de la nao"), Juan de la Cosa, for the catastrophe (Columbus 1982, 97). While Cosa seeks help from the caravel *La Niña,* Columbus has the *Santa María* dismantled and repurposed, with its mast and other pieces used to build the fort La Navidad, thus planting the imperial presence on foreign soil. In a sense, the wood fragment inhabited three imperial spaces: the ship (now dismantled), a fort (burned down by the indigenous tribe in 1493), and now a tomb with the remains of the admiral, who represents the Crown of Spain and its imperial aspirations.

All three spaces are heterotopias as conceived by Michel Foucault in "Of Other Spaces." If utopia is a society in a perfect form, an unreal space that accords with the traditional idyllic spaces in literary fiction and works of art, a heterotopia, by contrast, is an actual place that is set apart, self-contained like a museum, a school, or a prison, each possessing its distinctive code of conduct. For Foucault, the ultimate heterotopia is a ship: "If we think, after all, that the boat is a floating piece of space, a place without a place, that exists by itself, that is closed in on itself and at the same time is given over to the infinity of the sea and that, from port to port, … it goes as far as the colonies in search of the most precious treasures … The ship is the heterotopia par excellence" (1986, 27). The sonnet's *Santa María* is such a place of otherness, a self-contained space sailing on the "salty sea," a place "that exists by itself," "closed in on itself." Given to the infinity of the sea and wind, the ship goes in search of treasures. The wood fragment, standing for the ship, celebrates itself as having owned an empire and, attributing to itself the act of exploration and discovery, as having opened the way through uncharted waters to an unknown world. It ascribes to itself the space of empire and even the imperial quest ("senda abrí al Antártico hemisfero"), an allusion to Magellan's future circumnavigation through the Strait of Magellan to reach the Spice Islands. Now, however, literally dead in another heterotopia, in the realm of the entombed, but not wanting to be forgotten, the wood fragment writes its autobiography. It recalls its earlier days in the forest as a beech tree decked with leaves. Used as wood for sailing ships – especially for oars and masts – and for musical instruments, it acquired a voice to accompany singers: "del [haya] ... alas hice en mi jornada, / lenguas para cantar hice primero." From the carefree forest, it became an instrument of voice and voyage, coming to its ultimate rest deep within the tomb it now shares with Columbus.

Speaking from the tomb, imagined as a discursive site in the tradition of ancient tomb poems, the wood fragment proclaims the admiral a sacred presence: "Acompaño esta tumba tristemente, / y aunque son de Colón estos despojos, / su nombre callo, venerable y santo" (Mournfully, I accompany this tomb, and though Columbus's remains / lie here, his holy and venerable given name / I will not say). It refuses to state his holy name, that is, Christopher, an implicit identification of Columbus with his namesake, Saint Christopher, who carried the Christ child across the waters. From 1501, Columbus signed his name Christoferens, the carrier or bearer of Christ, assigning to himself a providential role in the discovery of America, the one who carried Christ across the oceans to a "New Heaven and a New Earth," as he wrote in his *Libro de las profecías* (1501–5).[9] Fray Bartolomé de las Casas, for whom the discovery had been a product of a divine mandate that rested on the name Christopher, confirms Columbus's assertion in his *Historia de las Indias*:

> Llamose, pues, por nombre Cristóbal, conviene a saber *Christum ferens*, que quiere decir traedor o llevador de Cristo, y así se firmaba él algunas veces; como en la verdad él haya sido el primero que abrió las puertas deste mar Océano, por donde entró y él metió a estas tierras tan remotas y reinos hasta entonces tan incógnitos a nuestro salvador Jesucristo y a su bendito nombre, el cual fué digno que antes que otro diese noticia de Cristo y hiciese adorar a estas innúmeras y tantos siglos olvidadas naciones. (1965, 1:28)

> (He was called Christopher, that is to say *Christum ferens*, which means bearer or carrier of Christ, and he sometimes signed this way, since he was the first to open the doors of the [Atlantic] Ocean, where he entered

> and brought to these remote lands and kingdoms until then unknown our saviour Jesus Christ and his holy name; he was worthy of bringing news of Christ and made him be worshipped by these numerous and for centuries forgotten nations.)

If the holy allows for participation in the veneration of a saint-like figure, it also allows for participation in a material ritual culture, a cult of relics. Writing on the holy in the Christian and Byzantine tradition of relics, Jaś Elsner comments, "The holy lies in its passage into a hidden space whose existence was announced and access to which was enabled through material framing and visual representation" (2015, 13). The tomb from which the voice speaks is a hidden, sacred space, a reliquary that encases the holy, for Columbus's "despojos" (remains) are, in effect, relics. The bit of wood, a fragment of the ship and a survivor that now lies with the explorer's remains, is also, by association, a hallowed object. The "pasajero" (wayfarer) becomes a pilgrim, and Columbus's tomb a pilgrimage site. But the wood fragment keeps Columbus's name hidden in order to prevent emotional experiences at the tomb: "de miedo que, de lástima, la gente / tanta agua ha de verter con tiernos ojos, / que al mar nos vuelva a entrambos con el llanto" (fearing that out of pity, tender eyes will shed so much water that we both will be washed out to sea again), as if proposing that if forgetting is a condition of memory, physical obliteration is a condition of material inscription, which is always subject to erasure.

The fragment's fear of erasure, of losing its ability to converse with the present, illustrates the force of Michel de Certeau's "practiced place," "a site activated by movements, narratives, actions and signs." As "spatial practices (rituals, pilgrimages)" activate the place, "it may become the object of imaginary renderings" (Mitchell, [1994] 2002, x–xi). The fragment, ensconced in the tomb, fears the instability introduced by the visitor, who travels in the mobile space of pilgrimage. The tomb – fixed, enclosed, stable – is a place of safety and refuge, of remembrance and recollection. But as a site of pilgrimage, a sacred space for the veneration of Columbus, it faces instability and danger, since the tears shed by pilgrims might return both Columbus and the wood fragment to the sea and its uncertainties.

Columbus is silent, a relic without agency. It is his companion who speaks out, who relates his personal history, who expresses his fear of erasure, and who seeks to preserve memory through speaking to the living, the "pasajero." Pilgrims visiting the tomb keep memory of the dead alive, making it a site of memory on terra firma; yet their tears threaten to destabilize the monument, returning it and the entombed to the sea, erasing its epitaph and its voice, and ending all conversation.[10]

Osuna's Marble Tomb

The sonnet epitaph on the marble tomb of Pedro Téllez Girón, the third duke of Osuna (1574–1624), is an elegy, celebrating his role as warrior. Osuna was, among other things, the second marquis of Peñafiel, the seventh count of Ureña, and the viceroy of Sicily (1611–16) and of Naples (1616–20). He fought mutineers in Flanders and in expeditions against the Turks and Barbary pirates in the Mediterranean. Quevedo, who served as his secretary and confidant during the duke's stint as viceroy of Naples, cast his praise as a memorial that was inscribed with words spoken by the marble itself:

Epitafio del sepulcro y con las armas del proprio
Habla el mármol
Memoria soy del más glorioso pecho
que España en su defensa vio triunfante;
en mí podrás, amigo caminante,
un rato descansar del largo trecho.
Lágrimas de soldados han deshecho
en mí las resistencias de diamante;
yo cierro al que el ocaso y el levante
a su victoria dio círculo estrecho.
Estas armas, vïudas de su dueño,
que visten de funesta valentía
este, si humilde, venturoso leño,
del grande Osuna son; él las vestía,
hasta que, apresurado el postrer sueño,
le ennegreció con noche el blanco día. (1:445–6)

(The epitaph to the tomb, with Osuna's armour
The marble speaks
I am memory of the most glorious man
that Spain saw triumphant in its defence;
here you can, my friend traveller,
rest for a while from such long journey.
Soldiers' tears have softened
my diamond-like hardness;
I enclose him who gave a narrow circle in his
triumph from East to West.
The armour, bereft of its owner,
which dresses with ill-fated courage

this fortunate, though humble, casket,
belongs to the great Osuna; he wore it,
until, untimely death brought
the darkness of night to his white day.)

The marble ascribes to itself the eminent role of memory, "Memoria soy" (I am memory), as if it were an archive of Osuna's past. It asserts its agency in the tradition of ancient tomb poems by retrieving through an act of voicing what is inscribed on its surface. Like Columbus's tomb, the marble tomb is a site of pilgrimage, activated by the "caminante," literally the walker, the pilgrim who is invited to rest from his long journey.[11] Pilgrims, identified as soldiers, paying homage to the loyal defender of Spain, keep Osuna's memory alive, wearing away the marble with tears of mourning.

Osuna's armour, the subject of the tercets, dresses the casket within the tomb as the material sign of his heroism and courage in combat. Its importance is signalled in the title and implicitly in the first two lines of the sonnet in the synecdoche "glorioso pecho" (glorious chest) and "defensa [de España]." As Quevedo's mouthpiece, the marble is both funereal and political, voicing the military virtues of a loyal friend, a famed Spanish warrior who died in prison after falling out of favour with the royal court – hinted at in the sonnet's "funesta valentía" (ill-fated courage].

Quevedo dedicated three other sonnet epitaphs to Osuna, testimonies of his deep affection for the duke, exalting in verse someone who had served his country with courage and distinction. These poems attest to Quevedo's loyalty to Osuna, despite the duke's arrogance, sense of self-entitlement, and above all his aggressive interventionist foreign policy, which clashed with the pacifist policies (Pax Hispanica) of Phillip III and his *valido*, the Duke of Lerma.[12] Osuna's boldest move was to send ships to confront the Venetian armada in the Adriatic. Accused of being involved in the conspiracy against Venice in 1618 (la conjuración de Venecia), "the viceroy ... and the Spanish ambassador to Venice, allegedly attempted to coordinate an armed takeover of the Venetian republic," an accusation likely advanced by Venice's propaganda (Mackenney 2002, 185).[13] On returning to Spain in 1620, Osuna faced charges, ranging from financial corruption at the Neapolitan court to sexual misconduct. Seven days after the king's death in 1621 he was placed under house arrest and three years later died in disgrace. To Quevedo, Spain had betrayed Osuna. In his sonnet epitaph "Memoria inmortal de don Pedro Girón, duque de Osuna, muerto en prisión" (Inmortal memory of don Pedro Girón, Duke of Osuna, dead in prison) he writes, "Faltar pudo su patria al grande Osuna, / pero no a su defensa sus hazañas; / diéronle muerte y cárcel las Españas, / de quien él hizo esclava la Fortuna" (1:425; His country may have failed the great Osuna, / but never did his deeds in its defence; / Spain gave him death and prison, / though he made Fortune its slave).[14]

Quevedo's speaking tombs demand to be present, to be heard through their inscribed words in order to preserve the memory of those who otherwise would be misremembered or forgotten. Both speakers, Columbus's wood companion and Osuna's marble slab, voice their own narratives as participants in the lives they commemorate. As active material intermediaries between the dead and the living, they are central actors in Quevedo's conversation project.

The Agency of a Paintbrush

In the *silva* "Al pincel" Quevedo extends his explorations of the agency of material objects through a series of apostrophes to a learned paintbrush that celebrates its skill in displaying image, emotion, and speech in canvas paintings, portrait miniatures, and hieroglyphs. Like books and tombs, the brush mediates between the living and the dead. In Titian's learned hand it gives a second life to a mysterious sultana, whose portrait initiates a dialogue between Islamic East and European West. In Ricci's hand, equally learned, the brush paints a portrait miniature for a love exchange. The brush also casts emotions on canvas and speaks the silent tongue of the ancient Egyptians. It dares even, the poet claims, to paint like God. For Quevedo, the agency of the paintbrush ultimately resides in its capacity to supersede nature, to overcome time and distance, and to retrieve the past.

Master of Nature and Time

"Al pincel" begins by conferring special authority on the object with a "tiny body":

> Tú, si en cuerpo pequeño,
> eres, pincel, competidor valiente
> de la Naturaleza,
> hácete el Arte dueño
> de cuanto crece y siente. (1:401.1–5)

(You, paintbrush,
despite your tiny body,
are nature's valiant rival;
art makes you master
of all that grows and feels.)

Rivalry or *paragone* between media was a hallmark of early modern art theory and practice: between painting and sculpture, the visual arts and music, Florentine design and Venetian colour, painting and poetry, and nature and art, with art defeating nature by surpassing it, a commonplace in Renaissance pictorialism (Hagstrum [1958] 1987, 81–8). Bembo's epitaph on Raphael – "Nature feared that she would be conquered while he lived, and would die when he died" – was a typical example of this conceit (81).[15]

In celebrating the paintbrush as the rival of nature, and its master, Quevedo relies on his knowledge of contemporary art theory, as he rehearses the illusionistic practices of painting in its use of colour and the deception of the senses, especially vision.[16] The deception of painting declared by Leon Battista Alberti in his influential *De pictura* (1435), with its geometrical rules as theoretical foundation of perspective, and the eye positioned as master of the visual field, is developed by later theorists, like Bernardino Daniello in *La Poetica* (1536) and Luis Alfonso de Carvallo in *Cisne de Apolo* (1602), who argue that the painter not only imitates nature but perfects it. Quevedo's contemporary Edmund Spenser offers a telling example of how art's pictorial effects make nature more "alluring," more "sensuous," in one word "better": "And [grapes] amongst, some were of burnisht gold, / So made by art, to beautifie the rest" (*The Faerie Queene*, 2.12.55) (Hagstrum [1958] 1987, 84). Along similar lines, in Góngora's *Polifemo*, objects of nature are made more luminous and beautiful, strikingly in the artificial display of the fruit in the Cyclops's bag, as if it were an ekphrastic rendition of a still life (see chapter 3). In "Al pincel," in the hands of two ancient portraitists, Protogenes and Apelles, the brush brings a second birth ("con nuevo parto de ingeniosa vida," 1:402.32) to dead emperors and kings. Ultimately, nature concedes defeat to the "learned brush, who taught it, / on a fine stretched canvas, / how to improve what it had made" (docto pincel, que la enseñaste, / en sutil lino estrecho, / cómo hiciera mejor lo que había hecho; 1:402.58–60).

Master of nature, "of all that grows and feels," Quevedo's paintbrush is also the master of time, retrieving the past in image, and enabling the living to communicate with those beyond memory:

[...] Eres tan fuerte,
eres tan poderoso,

que en desprecio del Tiempo y de sus leyes,
[... ... ...]
restituyes los príncipes y reyes,
la ilustre majestad y la hermosura
que huyó de la memoria sepultada.
Por ti, por tus conciertos
comunican los vivos con los muertos. (1:401–402.9–11, 14–18)

([...] you are so strong,
you are so mighty
that disdaining time's laws,
[... ... ...]
you restore, princes and kings,
illustrious majesty and beauty,
which fled from memory.
Through you, through your concerts
the living communicate with the dead.)

The apostrophized paintbrush rescues on panel and canvas the traces of those who have "fled from memory," echoing Alberti's observation in *De pictura* that painting makes the "absent present." The preservation of the past, painted on the material surface, involves an interactive performance. In Mieke Bal's terms, the experience of viewing a painting becomes itself an event, "an action carried out by an *I* in relation to what the work takes as *you*" (Bryson, quote from Bal, 2001, 5; emphasis in the original). "Conciertos" takes us there: "Por ti, por tus conciertos, comunican los vivos con los muertos." *Conciertos* – from the verb *concertar*, "to arrange" – conceives the brush as an active agent, alive and empowered, staged to connect the living, the viewer, with the painted image of the dead. In a subtle and profound sense, *conciertos* – meaning "simultaneous voices in song" (*Diccionario de Autoridades*) – foregrounds the dialogue between the viewer and the painted presences, and the harmony created by their mutual interaction. That suggestive musical language inspired both the meditation on reading the ancients through their voices in the sonnet "Desde la Torre" and the image of *conciertos* in "Al pincel" for a fruitful conjoining of the musical and the visual arts.

The Learned Brush

Like the sonnet's "libros doctos," which bring the voices of the past to the present, the learned brush ("docto pincel") in Titian's hand brings to life a lovely sultana, giving her a second life in paint. Within a baroque poetics the epithet *docto* typically denotes the classical learning of those who practise the *poesía culta* of the period. But *docto* also has a specific meaning within contemporary pictorial theory. In his *Diálogos de la pintura* (*Dialogues on Painting,* 1633), Vicente Carducho selects "saber" (knowledge) and "estudio" (study) as indispensable steps for achieving a "docta pintura" (learned painting). Polish, care, and reason characterize the "pintores doctos," writes Carducho: "Los doctos, que pintan acabadísimo, y perfilado, obran con cuidado y razon todas las cosas, y Ticiano fue uno dellos en su principio, siguiendo a Iuan Belino su primer Maestro, y después con borrones hizo cosas admirables" (1979, 261). (The learned, who paint fully and with much polish, work with care and reason in all things, and Titian was one of them at the beginning of his career, following Giovanni Bellini, his first teacher, and later from preliminary sketches he executed admirable things.)

Quevedo, too, places Titian among the *doctos* in whose hand the brush executes current artistic codes in a singular manner, especially the deception inherent in the painter's art and its superseding of nature. He singles out Titian's portrait of Sultana Rosa, wife of Suleyman the Magnificent, sultan of the Ottoman Empire (r. 1520–66):

Ya se vio muchas veces,
¡oh pincel poderoso!, en docta mano
mentir almas los lienzos de Ticiano.
Entre sus dedos vimos
nacer segunda vez, y más hermosa,
aquella sin igual gallarda Rosa,
que tantas veces de la fama oímos.
Dos le hizo de una,
y dobló lisonjero su cuidado
al que, fiado en bárbara fortuna,
traía, por diadema, media luna
del cielo, a quien ofende coronado. (1:403.67–78)

(Already many times, O mighty brush,
by Titian's learned hand, we have seen
a canvas feign men's souls.
Between his fingers we saw
born again, and more beautifully,
that peerless, elegant Rosa,
whose fame everyone knew.

From one he made two,
and doubled the sweet sorrow
for him, who trusting barbaric fortune,
wore, as the crowning blow,
the horns of the half moon.)

The term *docta* is linked to the excellence of the paintbrush in technique, its skill (as Carducho observed), and here its ability to deceive (feign souls ["mentir almas"]), as it creates in Titian's hand a life-like portrait of the sultana. Rehearsing the notion of the mastery of art over nature, Titian's brush "improves" upon Rosa's image, making her even more beautiful in her painterly birth ("vimos / nacer segunda vez"). As the carrier and performer of pictorial codes, the brush – painting the woman "que tantas veces de la fama oímos" (whose fame everyone knew) – implicitly initiates a dialogue in the complex, often turbulent theatre of cultural and political encounters between Islamic East and European West.

Rosa, who became a fixture in the European imaginary, as much legend as history, was the product of a colourful telling. Said to have been born in Ukraine, she was taken captive by Crimean Tartars sometime between 1515 and 1520 and ended up at a slave market in Istanbul, where she was bought by the grand vizier Ibrahim Pasha for the imperial harem of Crown Prince Suleyman, who became sultan in 1520 (Yermolenko 2010, 2). Given the name Hurrem (Turkish for "Joyful" or "Laughing One") because of her cheerful nature, she was called in European accounts variously Rossa, Rosselana, Roxolana, or Roxelana. The West was as fascinated with Rosa as was Suleyman, who married her against established custom, to the shock of the Ottomans and Westerners alike (Yermolenko 2010, 6). Her image became popular in Spain, especially through Titian's painting and in references to it in Lope de Vega's plays *La Santa Liga* (1621) and *La Dorotea* (1633) (de Armas 1996).[17]

The only extant painting of Rosa connected to Titian, *La Sultana Rossa*, by one of his followers, or a copy of Titian's original, is housed in the John and Mable Ringling Museum of Art (Sarasota, Florida) (fig. 1.1). She appears "wearing a striped green and gold gown with short sleeves, a pearl necklace (a Western artifact) and richly jeweled high pointed headdress (Eastern in origin); in her left hand she holds a marten with a collar around its neck" (Suida 1949, 59). A rose tucked in her bosom could be a play with her name, suggesting that the painting was intended as an ideal representation of the Sultana (Wethey 1971, 205).[18]

Rosa's portrait was animated by a seduction of the exotic in European cultural circles, especially in Venice, which had strong commercial

Figure 1.1 *La Sultana Rossa*, c. 1552, oil on canvas. Copy after Titian. The John and Mable Ringling Museum of Art, Sarasota, Florida.

and artistic ties with the Ottoman Empire. Titian, a favorite of the Habsburgs, had at least an indirect contact with the Ottomans through his mentor, Giovanni Bellini (1430–1516), whose brother Gentile Bellini (1429–1507) was a painter in Istanbul at the court of Mehmed II, who advocated close cultural relations with the West (Jardine and Brotton 2000). Beyond acknowledging the lure of the exotic, the *silva* recalls long-standing political and religious conflicts between Habsburg Spain and the Ottomans, in which Suleyman stood as the supreme adversary. For the Sultan, alluded to only briefly in the poem as "al que," Quevedo invents a diadem fashioned from the crescent moon ("traía, por diadema, media luna"), a Turkish emblem adopted from the Byzantine and often portrayed upturned. An ornamental headband was typically worn by Eastern rulers as a sign of royal status and prestige, but here it is transformed into an offensive headgear of metaphorical "horns," a sign of the betrayed husband, the "cornudo" (Cacho Casal 2012a, 108). The paintbrush is complicit in the mockery as it magnifies Rosa's beauty, doubled as she is painted ("dos le hizo de una"), while doubling the Sultan's sorrow ("y dobló lisonjero su cuidado"). Quevedo diminishes him further in an oblique reference to his heathen practices: "fiado en bárbara fortuna / […] ofende [al cielo] coronado" (trusting in barbarous fortune / […], crowned, he offends heaven).

Quevedo's imagined diadem invites his learned reader to recall another headgear, the actual crown helmet that Suleyman wore in his march to Vienna in 1532 to confront Holy Roman Emperor Charles V, in what amounted to a material staging of the political rivalries between East and West (fig.1.2).[19] Designed and manufactured by Venetian artisans, that spectacular helmet stood for the sultan's challenge to Charles and to Pope Clement VII, who wore similar but smaller crowns in their joint procession after Charles's coronation by the pope in Bologna in 1530 (fig. 1.3).

"Within the context of Habsburg-Ottoman-papal rivalry," writes Gülru Necipoğlu, the crown, a non-Islamic object, was staged to communicate "Ottoman imperial claims to a European audience through a Western discourse of power" (1989, 401). Publicized by Venetian woodcuts and the much-copied engraving of Agostino Veneziano, as well as by pamphlets, plays, and songs, the crown helmet along with other lavish ceremonial objects won the sultan his title of "Magnificent" in the West (Necipoğlu 1989, 418–19).[20] Quevedo's home-grown diadem imprinted with the half-moon satirizes Suleyman's extravagant crown in order to humiliate the Habsburg's archenemy. The paintbrush, in Titian's hand, rehearses those still-powerful rivalries between East

Figure 1.2 Agostino Veneziano, *Sultan Suleyman the Magnificent Wearing the Venetian Helmet*, 1535, engraving. The Elisha Whittelsey Fund. © The Metropolitan Museum of Art/Art Resource, New York.

Figure 1.3 Nicholas Hogenberg (c. 1500–39), *Entry of Pope Clement VII and Emperor Charles V into Bologna after His Coronation as Emperor on 24 February 1530*. Plate 27, c. 1530, etching. Bpk Bildagentur/Art Resource, New York.

and West through its portrait of a sultana who has crossed cultural boundaries.

An Object of Exchange

The paintbrush can initiate an equally fruitful dialogue through the miniature portrait of a beautiful beloved named Lícida, attributed to the late Mannerist and early baroque painter Giovanni Battista Ricci (1537–1627). Called *retratico, retrato de faltriquera* (pocket portrait), or simply *naipe,* the miniature was in its portability the ultimate performative object, ubiquitous in aristocratic circles from the mid-sixteenth century (Colomer 2002, 65–6). Exquisitely painted and sometimes deceptively, these "portraits in little" were sent as gifts to friends, as enticements to prospective marriage partners, and as love tokens. They were worn as jewellery on necklaces and as rings, and they served as memorial portraits of the dead. As "wandering things," they both embodied the person portrayed and established a relationship with the recipient (Koos 2014). Lícida's miniature reads:

Por ti Richi ha podido,
docto, cuanto ingenioso,
en el rostro de Lícida hermoso,
con un naipe nacido,
criar en sus cabellos
oro, y estrellas en sus ojos bellos;
en sus mejillas, flores,
primavera y jardín de los amores;
y en su boca, las perlas,
riendo de quien piensa merecerlas.
Así que fue su mano,
con trenzas, ojos, dientes y mejillas,
Indias, cielo y verano,
escondiendo aun más altas maravillas,
o de invidioso de ellas
o de piedad del que llegase a vellas. (1:403–4.85–100)

(Through you Ricci was able,
as witty as he was learned,
to frame Lícida's beautiful face,
born on her *miniature portrait,*
gold in her hair,

and stars in her lovely eyes;
on her cheeks, flowers,
a Spring and garden of love
and in her mouth, pearls,
mocking whoever thinks he deserves them.
So crafted his hand,
with tresses, eyes, teeth, and cheeks,
heaven, summer, and the Indies;
hiding still greater marvels,
whether from jealousy or piety
that one might see them.)

For Quevedo, the miniature of Lícida painted by Ricci's brush, ostensibly as an object of courtship or exchange between lovers, celebrates the woman's lovely body parts by means of fetishes as in a blason of a Petrarchan lyric – gold for her hair, stars for her eyes, and pearls (the riches of the Indies) for her teeth. Like Rosa's image brought to life for a second time and "improved" in paint, the miniature magnifies the beauty of the absent Lícida. The miniature's transactional function is best captured by Samuel Johnson: "Miniature Art, so valuable in diffusing friendship, in reviving tenderness, in awakening the affections of the absent, and continuing the presence of the dead" (quoted in Stratton 1988, 15).

Embodied Emotions and Encoded Wisdom

If the paintbrush has the capacity to feign souls, making its subjects lifelike in portraits large and small, it also can show us their thoughts and affections, retreaving the past in image and paint:

Por ti el lienzo suspira
y sin sentidos mira.
Tú sabes sacar risa, miedo y llanto
de la ruda madera, y puedes tanto,
que cercas de ira negra las entrañas
de Aquiles, y amenazas con sus manos
de nuevo a los troyanos,
que, sin peligro y con ingenio, engañas.
Vemos por ti en Lucrecia
la desesperación, que el honor precia;
de su sangre cubierto
el pecho, sin dolor alguno abierto. (1:405.101–12)

(Through you the canvas sighs
and, though lacking sight, it sees.
You know how to extract laughter,
fear, and grief from coarse wood;
you can even fill the belly
of Achilles with black anger,
and with his hands threaten again Trojans,
whom you deceive without peril and with wit.
We see through you the despair
of Lucrecia, who prizes honor;
her breast covered with blood,
the cause of her woe hidden.)

The brush casts emotions on canvas through its artful deceit ("engañas"), endowing it with sight and feelings, extracting from coarse wood a range of emotions – laughter, fear, and grief – and implicitly engaging the spectator's own emotions. Inwardness portrayed materially as embodied passions or affections was a familiar figuration in contemporary works. Here the brush paints passions as part of the "fabric of the body," as early modern ontology dictates, blending psychology and physiology, in "a mind darkened by the burning of choler" (Paster 2004, 5, 36). It brings alive Achilles's all-consuming anger – his black rage teeming in his bowels ("entrañas") – and it once again threatens the Trojans with Achilles's own hands ("amenazas con sus manos / de nuevo a los troyanos"). It depicts the despair of Lucretia, who after being raped by Tarquin, her husband's fellow soldier, stabbed herself in the chest, which drips with blood as if despair itself were oozing from within. But in painting Lucretia, the brush saves her from oblivion: "En ti se deposita / lo que la ausencia y lo que el tiempo quita" (115–16; In you is kept safe what absence and time take away).

The paintbrush also speaks the silent tongue of the Egyptians, the visual signs that encode their wisdom:

Ya fue tiempo que hablaste,
y fuiste a los egipcios lengua muda.
Tú también enseñaste
en la primera edad, sencilla y ruda,
alta filosofía
en doctos hieroglíficos obscuros;
y los misterios puros
de ti la religión ciega aprendía. (1:406.117–24)

(Ages ago you spoke
and were for the Egyptians a mute tongue.
You also taught lofty philosophy
in that ancient time,
so simple and rude,
with obscure, learned hieroglyphs;
and blind religion
learned from your pure mysteries.)

The enthusiasm for Egyptian hieroglyphs nurtured by the visual arts (notably the Capitoline frieze and the obelisk of Rameses II, which was placed in Rome's Piazza Santa Maria del Popolo in 1589 and published by Nicolaus van Aelst [fig. 1.4]) and by written texts (like Horapollo's *Hyeroglyphica* and the enigmatic *Hypnerotomachia Poliphili*) was part of what has been called "the Egyptian Renaissance" (Curran 2007).[21] Reading hieroglyphs through a humanist perspective, Quevedo calls them "doctos" and ascribes to them "alta filosofía." As a visual script of "pure mysteries," which taught the "blind religion" of the ancients, hieroglyphs were a font of the secret knowledge and secret wisdom prefiguring Christian truths. "The hieroglyph fashion is an offshoot of *prisca theologia*," writes Frances Yates, "for it owed much of its vogue to the deep respect for Egyptian wisdom as exemplified in Hermes Trismegistus" ([1964] 1977, 163). Marsilio Ficino paid the deepest respect in translating the *Corpus Hermeticum* (1463; better known as the *Pimander*) attributed to Trismegistus, which Ficino claimed to be a foundational text for Christian revelation.[22] In speaking the mute tongue of the Egyptians, the tiny brush serves as the medium of transmission of hermetic philosophy, the instrument for conversations with a distant but still relevant civilization.

The *silva* ends with an extravagant apotheosis to the brush, the "usurper" that dares to paint like God, the *Deus artifex* or *Deus pictor*.[23] Called "breve punta" (a pointed hairbrush for applying colour), it is glorified for its singular talent:

Tuya la gloria es y los despojos,
pues, breve punta, en los colores crías
cuanto el sol en el suelo,
y cuanto en él los días,
y cuanto en ellos trae y lleva el cielo. (1:406.153–7)

(Yours is the glory and yours the spoils,
for, brief point, you create in colours

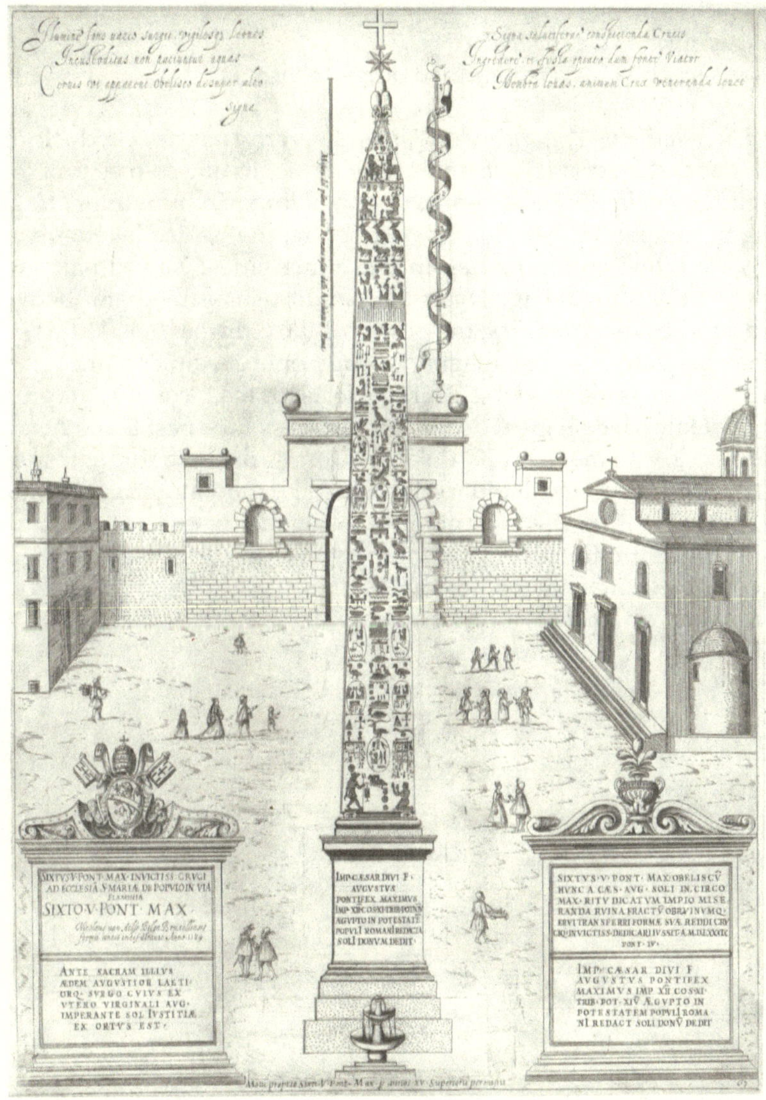

Figure 1.4 Nicolaus van Aelst (1550s–1613), *View of the Egyptian Obelisk of Rameses II from Heliopolis, Placed in Rome's Piazza Santa Maria del Popolo during the Pontificate of Sixtus V in 1589*, engraving and etching. *Speculum Romanae Magnificentiae*. British Museum, London. © The Trustees of the British Museum / Art Resource, New York.

as much as the sun on earth,
and as much as the sun in the days,
and as much as heaven brings and carries in them.)

The *Diccionario de Autoridades* defines the verb *criar* as "producir algo de la nada, dar ser a lo que antes no lo tenía, lo que solo es propio de la omnipotencia divina" (to produce something from nothing, to give being to something that did not exist before, that which belongs exclusively to divine omnipotence). In these final lines Quevedo alerts the reader to the ultimate agency of the paintbrush, as mediator between earth and heaven, imitating the power of the Creator.

The poems analysed in this chapter are prime examples of the ways in which agency is ascribed to cultural objects for the recovery and preservation of knowledge, great deeds, and images of the past that otherwise would be lost to memory. If books and tombs mediate through speech what lies in print and lapidary inscriptions, the paintbrush mediates images by creating the material means for their preservation on canvas, in portrait miniatures, and hieroglyphs. In each case the object is activated by human interaction, by readers, passers-by, and viewers. At the core of each poem is an encounter with memory as encoded in, and accessed through, the material.

Chapter Two

Material Rome

In April 1617 Francisco de Quevedo arrived in Rome on a diplomatic mission to Pope Paul V.[1] While wandering through the city in search of ancient Rome, what impressed Quevedo and inspired one of his best known *silvas*, "Roma antigua y moderna," were two sets of material remains – the ruined triumphal arches, bridges, and temples dotting the cityscape, and the rescued artefacts displayed in the Capitoline Museum, at the religious and political centre of ancient Rome. Quevedo's encounter with material Rome, with its vast archive of ruins and monuments, some relatively intact, others in various states of decay, evoked a complex cultural memory. For him, Rome was a layered text to be read in its ancient and modern guises.

Decoding that fractured landscape of ruins and displaced objects meant, in effect, to confront what the cultural geographer Carl Sauer called the "morphology of landscape," the relation between the physical landscape and its cultural impress ([1925] 1967). Quevedo was especially drawn to the ruins of the ancient infrastructure, which reflected the collapse of imperial Rome, and to the salvaged antiquities on the Capitoline, like the equestrian statue of Marcus Aurelius and the *Trophies of Marius*, which for him embodied the spirit and majesty of ancient Rome. The poem's narrative is not linear. Its temporal mapping is a free shifting of past and present, and its metric form (except for its first fourteen lines, which is a sonnet) is a *silva*, a stanza with unfixed rhyme and variable combinations of heptasyllables and hendecasyllables, allowing for metrical freedom and flexibility.[2] The poem owes as much to the discursive renderings of Rome in ancient and early modern texts, in particular the contemporary vernacular and neo-Latin poetry of ruins, as to the poet's direct viewing of Rome's material remains. The *silva* ends in the poet's own time, Catholic Rome, after the popes had refashioned the cityscape through urban renewal projects that made the papacy the authentic heir and guardian of Rome's imperial past. This chapter deals with the ways in which Quevedo's visual reading of the city's material remains combines with his readings of earlier textual fragments, interweaving monumental ruins, fractured antiquities, and museum artefacts to produce a complex memory of Rome.

Then and Now

Sigmund Freud, who was well informed about Rome and its history, offered an intriguing reading of its cityscape in his *Civilization and Its Discontents* (1930) that is useful in understanding Quevedo's own reading of material Rome. Freud invites the reader to imagine the city as being like the human mind, "in which nothing that has once come into existence will have passed away, and all the earliest phases of development continue to exist alongside the latest one."[3] In this imagined cityscape everything exists synchronously, as an archeological palimpsest, just as Freud understood memory to reside in the mind:

> This would mean that in Rome the palaces of the Caesars and the Septizonium of Septimus Severus would still be rising to their old height on the Palatine ... In the place occupied by the Palazzo Cafarelli would once more stand – without the Palazzo having to be removed – the Temple of Jupiter Capitolinus ... On the Piazza of the Pantheon we should find not only the Pantheon of today, as it was bequeathed to us by Hadrian, but, on the same site, the original edifice erected by Agrippa; indeed, the same piece of ground would be supporting the church of Santa Maria sopra Minerva and the ancient temple over which it was built. (Freud 2005, 44)

Freud ultimately rejected the analogy between the human mind and Rome's built environment because urban spaces, once created, are destroyed, repurposed, and replaced in the normal course of events. Catharine Edwards offers an important insight into Freud's imagery that is relevant here. She finds that in conjoining time and place, Freud posits "an image of place as time made visible" (Edwards 1996, 28). It is what Mikhail Bakhtin, in his notion of the chronotope, observes in narratives, that time "thickens, takes on flesh, becomes artistically visible" (1989, 28). Freud's vision "seems to erode historical differentiation," remarks Edwards, a strategy that is suggestively close to the way in which influential Roman writers, notably Livy in his *History* and Virgil in the *Aeneid*, envisioned Rome's past, with places and monuments serving as repositories of memory, resulting in a kind of non-sequential history in which the past is experienced through place (Edwards 28–9, 43). For Quevedo, too, Rome is a layered landscape, with the past manifest in place and in material objects, and best understood not chronologically but in a juxtaposition of a then and a now.

The *silva* shifts between discursive and temporal registers, between speaking voices, and between material stagings. In the preliminary stanzas a third-person narrator guides a "huésped" (guest) through imperial Rome as he offers a visual reading of the cityscape in which he contrasts Rome's imperial present with its pastoral past:

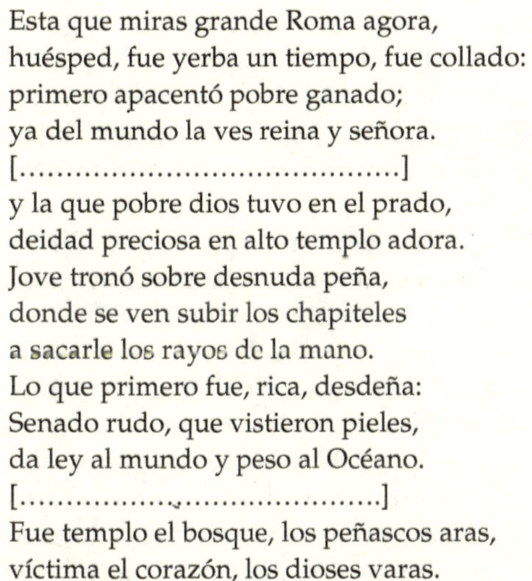
Esta que miras grande Roma agora,
huésped, fue yerba un tiempo, fue collado:
primero apacentó pobre ganado;
ya del mundo la ves reina y señora.
[...]
y la que pobre dios tuvo en el prado,
deidad preciosa en alto templo adora.
Jove tronó sobre desnuda peña,
donde se ven subir los chapiteles
a sacarle los rayos de la mano.
Lo que primero fue, rica, desdeña:
Senado rudo, que vistieron pieles,
da ley al mundo y peso al Océano.
[...]
Fue templo el bosque, los peñascos aras,
víctima el corazón, los dioses varas. (1:262.1–4, 7–14, 23–4)

(This great Rome that you see now, guest,
was at one time grass, it was hill:
first it fed the poor herd;
now you see it queen and lady of the world.
[...]
and the city with a modest god in the meadow,
now adores a precious deity in a high temple.
Jove thundered above a naked peak
where the capitals are now seen rising
to take the lightning from his hands.
Now rich, it disdains what it once was:
A rude Senate once dressed in animal hides,
now dictates laws to the world and gives weight to the Ocean.
[...]
The forest was a temple, the rocks were altars,
the heart, a victim, the gods were wooden idols.)[4]

Casting the city in terms of a pastoral then and a built now, the narrator rehearses the Roman concept of memory as anchored in place and in the material. "Roman memory was rooted in the sacred ground of the city," writes Florence Dupont. "To walk around Rome was to travel through its memory, past Romulus' cabin, Cacus' rock and Egeria's wood" (1992, 74). Livy, Propertius, and Virgil saw Rome's history through its topography, as did Petrarch, a writer closer in time to Quevedo and of enormous influence in early modern Spanish literary production. In a letter to his friend Giovanni Colonna reminiscing on their wanderings through Rome's ruins, Petrarch projects events from Roman history taken chiefly from Virgil and Livy onto the landscape: "at each step there was present something which would excite our tongue and mind: here was the palace of Evander, there the shrine of Carmentis, here the cave of Cacus, there the famous she-wolf and the fig-tree of Rumina with the more apt surname of Romulus."[5]

Like Petrarch, who reads Rome's fourteenth-century ruins through its ancient authors, Quevedo follows a well-rehearsed script, reading monuments and their remains through written texts. The *silva*'s narrative voice in these first stanzas views imperial Rome through a textual memory largely supplied by Propertius. Writing in the time of Augustus, the elegiac poet praises the imposing imperial cityscape to a visitor ("hospes"). He follows what Alain Gowing notes about the way in which writers of the Augustan period captured history materially and temporally: "Building projects such as the Forum of Augustus furnished stunning, persuasive, visual prompts to induce the viewer to make the connection between past and present" (2005, 19). Propertius cites the built environment but adds details to explain to his "viewer" the connections between a humble past and an imperial present:

> All that you see here, visitor, where mighty Rome now stands, was grass and hill before the coming of Phrygian Aeneas; and where stands the Palatine sacred to Apollo of the Ships, lay the cattle of Evander the exile. These golden temples were built for gods of clay, who deemed it no shame that their huts were crudely built. Tarpeian Jupiter thundered from a bare rock, and the Tiber was an alien to our cattle. Where now stands the house above a flight of stairs [the temple of Romulus on the Quirinal], the house of Remus; a single hearth was the mighty kingdom of two brothers. The Curia, which now stands high and resplendent with its hem-frocked senate, then housed a rustic company of Fathers clad in skins. (2006, 4.1.1–12; emended)

The *silva*'s narrator assumes the voice of Propertius's ancient Roman, who is speaking to the pilgrim visiting the imperial city, but the voice might well have been Quevedo's own, artfully displaced in time to imperial Rome and addressing himself in a fictive doubling as the "huésped." If imperial Rome is Propertius's present, it is in effect Quevedo's past, recreated and recuperated through a textual memory, a past that he later will find embodied in the city's ruins and in the artefacts of the Capitoline.

What catches the reader's attention in Quevedo's preliminary lines, where the narrator contrasts Rome's humble origins with its later imperial glory, is the monumental architecture, which is sketched against a primitive landscape, with man-made objects supplanting nature, as in Propertius's "past rusticity and present urbanity." A "pobre dios" (modest god) worshiped in the fields, later reinforced by "los dioses varas" – the gods were wooden idols, a reference to earlier Etruscan structures built on the Capitoline[6] – becomes splendid statuary, "deidad preciosa en alto templo" (a precious deity in a high temple). Jupiter, the god of thunder and lighting, is raised from a "bare rock" to a temple of mighty capitals ("chapiteles"), referring to the temple of Jupiter Optimus Maximus, the most important shrine on the Capitoline Hill in imperial Rome. Burned down in 83 BCE and rebuilt magnificently with marble and gold, it "could be made to stand for the city as a whole and even for the entire Roman empire" (Edwards 1996, 70). Temples, monuments, and tall buildings transformed the landscape. Implicit here is majesty ("majestad"), which Quevedo later invokes to describe the objects "saved" in the Capitoline by a personified Rome. Admiring descriptions of Rome's built environment anticipate the narrator's conversations with the city through its ruins and artefacts. The cityscape, in Denis Cosgrove's words, "provides a stage for human action, and, like a theatre set, [plays] a highly visible role in the performance" (1993, 1).

Quevedo prefaces his exploration of Rome's cityscape by viewing the formation of empire through the conquest of rivers. Here the Tiber is linked to Rome's prehistory, to Evander, a Greek Arcadian hero who is said to have brought the gods, the alphabet, and the laws to Italy and to have founded Pallantium near the river where Rome would stand: "A la sed the los bueyes / de Evandro fugitivo, Tibre santo / sirvió" (1:262.27–9; To the thirst of exiled Evander's cattle the holy Tiber served). "Consuls" and "kings" then tainted the Tiber with blood in their quest for territorial expansion, enchaining foreign rivers – the Danube, the Rhine, the Ebro, the Hebrus, the Tagus, and the Nile (33–7). Quevedo may have been recalling the Roman triumphs, extravagant spectacles that staged the defeat of its enemies: victorious generals returning from war paraded prisoners in chains, who marched along with personifications of associated rivers, which were also in chains, sometimes on floats, bore their names, and served as metonyms for their lands. "In the triumph," writes Ida Östenberg, "the city constituted the stage that set the event and defined the procession as a civic concern" (2009, 13). Staged materially, the triumph was a ritual performance, at once religious and political, that created collective memory, both reflecting and reinforcing a sense of community, which in turn confirmed and shaped Roman identity.[7]

In his description of Caesar's imagined first triumph over Gallia in 46 BCE, Lucan writes in the *Pharsalia* of "Caesar fitting chains to Rhine and Channel [Oceanus], Caesar's lofty war-chariot followed by Gallic chieftains" (1993, 3.76–8). Ovid in the *Ars amatoria* mentions defeated rivers: "That is Euphrates, his forehead fringed with reeds; he with the dark blue locks down-hanging will be Tigris" (1969, 1.223–4). In the *Tristia* he writes of the conquered Rhine paraded in an imagined triumph: "This thing with broken horns and sorry covering of green sedge was the Rhine himself, discoloured with his own blood" (1996, 4.2.41–4).[8] Propertius famously cites the Nile flowing humbly to Rome with its seven captive streams (mouths), along with "the necks of kings bound with chains of gold" (2006, 2.1.31–3), images that Quevedo combined to construct a baroque conceit of the Nile as a hydra with seven mouths and seven necks, of crystal and silver, to evoke the beauty and terror of the bejewelled river as the mythical serpentine monster: "el que por siete bocas derramado, / y de plata y cristal hidra espumante, / con siete cuellos hiere el mar sonante" (1:263.43–5). As emblems of conquered lands and peoples, rivers situated on the edges of Rome's territories anchored materially "the worldwide domination of Rome," its global conquest (Östenberg 2009, 234). "Their display as captives transmitted a clear message that their formerly fierce and unrestrained powers had been tamed and brought under Roman control," writes Östenberg; "Civilization now mastered Nature."

Reading Ruins

As the *silva* unfolds, it passes from Rome's imperial past to the post-imperial present of the wandering "huésped," whose reading of the Tiber locates it within a space of ruination. Formerly elegant bridges, signs of imperial might, now lie in ruins:

Añudaron al Tibre cuello y frente
puentes en lazos de alabastro puros,

sobre peñascos duros,
llorando tantos ojos su corriente,
que aun parecen, en campo de esmeralda,
las puentes Argos y pavón la espalda. (1:263.50–5)

(Bridges with ornaments of pure alabaster
tied the Tiber, neck and forehead,
over hard rocks,
so many eyes crying out its current
that on a field of emerald,
the bridges still look like Argus and a peacock's back.)

In imperial times, bridge-building was a mark of civilization, a sign of mastery over nature, and by extension of military triumph. In Statius's *Silvae*, book 4, the victory of Domitian is defined by the personified Volturnus River, which rises up and tells the triumphant Roman emperor, "you are supreme lord and conqueror of my bank" (Kleiner 1991, 185). But in Quevedo's *silva*, nature masters civilization, the undoing of Rome's magnificent bridges signalling the fall of empire. The arches of the bridges, perceived as eyes crying, that is, generating the river's currents ("llorando tantos ojos su corriente"), lie on the green grass of the riverbanks, its field of emerald ("campo de esmeralda"). The scene of ruination is animated by two baroque conceits based on Ovid's tale of Argus and the peacock: Juno places the eyes of her spy, the hundred-eyed Argus killed by Mercury, on the feathers of her bird, the peacock (Ovid 1984, 1:1.722–3). In Quevedo's text the peacock's "eyes" set on their green-feathered background allow for their metaphorical connection to the arches (eyes) of the collapsed bridges that are scattered on the green riverbanks, and the peacock, the most spectacular of birds, mediates between the ruins and the natural landscape. Baroque images rescue the fallen bridges, if for an instance, from the sense of total devastation.

Georg Simmel's theory of ruins reinforces the rescue of this visual rhetoric of bridges collapsed on riverbanks, of ancient Rome's architecture overtaken by nature. For Simmel, in a scene of ruins, it is architecture, the product of the human spirit and the human will, that is dismantled by the "downward-dragging" power of nature as a corroding agent, resulting in a new aesthetic: a crumbling structure acquires new meaning as an artefact. "The ruin of a building," he writes, "means that where the work of art is dying, other forces and forms, those of nature, have grown; and that out of what of art still lives in the ruin and what of nature already lives in it, there has emerged a new whole, a characteristic unity" (1959, 260). Simmel continues, "So long as we can speak of a ruin at all and not of a mere heap of stones, [the power of nature] does not sink the work of man into the formlessness of mere matter ... Nature has transformed the work of art into material for her own expression, as she had previously served as material for art" (261–2). What fascinated Simmel about ruins, observes Svetlana Boym, was "a peculiar form of 'collaboration' between human and natural creation" (2010, 556). Quevedo's baroque poetics offers its own peculiar form of collaboration. As if rehearsing Simmel's paradigm, it meshes the arches and alabaster of the tumbled bridges, the emerald of the green riverbanks, and the peacock, a kind of living jewel in its beauty and splendour, to serve as materials for an aesthetic transformation. And here, following Simmel's line of thought, past and present come together within an irreducible tension in an act of delicate recuperation, of artistic triumph.

Artists sought in their own way to recuperate the built environment of ancient Rome through idealized reconstructions of "what classical Rome was believed to have looked like" (Saxl 1957, 1:205). An architectural fantasy ascribed to Luciano Laurana "shows a circular antique building in the centre," the round building considered by artists of the times as "the most perfect classical creation." The building's "wings [are] formed by palaces with open colonnades on the ground floor; the pavement is laid out with stones of different colours, so as to show the axis leading to the centre of the main building" (Saxl 1957, 1:205) (fig. 2.1). A stage design by Baldassare Peruzzi shows a combination of classical and modern buildings, some partly in ruins, recognizable among these being "the cupola of the Pantheon, ... the three columns of the Forum, the tomb of Hadrian, the Colosseum" (Saxl 1957, 1:205–6) (fig. 2.2).[9] Unlike Laurana, Peruzzi includes Rome's contemporary ruins as magnificent as the newly restored or newly constructed buildings, sketched as if the artist wanted to resurrect the spirit of the ancient structures, splendid even in their ruinous state.

The affirmation of ruins in Rome's cityscape had been recognized in another manner by Renaissance popes and Conservators, the civic administrators of the city, who undertook the preservation of the material remains of imperial Rome. In his bull of 1462 Pope Pius II, who along with the Conservators proclaimed himself guardian of the ancient city, advocated the preservation of ruins for their aesthetic beauty as well as material evidence of ancient virtues: "Not only the basilicas, churches, and religious sites, in which many relics of the saints reside, but also the ancient buildings and their ruins should be handed down

Figure 2.1 Luciano Laurana (attribution), *View of an Ideal City*. Galleria Nazionale delle Marche, Urbino. Scala/Art Resource, New York.

Figure 2.2 Baldassare Peruzzi (attribution), *Theatrical Perspective with Monuments of Rome*, mid-sixteenth century. Gabinetto dei Disegni e delle Stampe, Ufizzi Gallery, Florence. Scala/Art Resource, New York.

to posterity, as these confer upon the city its most beautiful adornment and its greatest charm; they attest to ancient virtues and encourage us to emulate their glorious example" (cited in Karmon 2011, 69). But the results were mixed, for the preservation was accompanied by the vast destruction of archaeological sites that, as David Karmon has observed, was driven by excavations for stone to supply new construction and by the looting and unearthing of artefacts by "antiquarian treasure hunters," including nobles and popes, to satisfy their insatiable desire for collecting antiquities.

Quevedo describes at length the ruination of the Roman cityscape with a certain nostalgia, exhibited by the wanderer, who projects his own feelings of loss onto the landscape.[10] The exaltation of collapsed bridges through baroque conceits turns into a reading of ruins as unmitigated devastation. The protective walls around the seven hills have been vanquished by time and are about to tumble. And the abandoned, crumbling temple of Janus lacks enough vegetation to sustain a harmonious, artistic construct (recalling Simmel's understanding of ruins): "en su templo y ara apenas / hay yerba que dé sombra a las arenas" (1:264.79–80; in his temple and altar there is hardly any grass to give shade to the sands). The ruined stone is but a sign of the irreversibility of time and the triumph of decay. The temple is on its way to becoming dust. The resonant "descansadas de los altos templos, / vuelven a ser riberas las riberas" (83–4; unburdened of their high temples, the riverbanks turn into riverbanks once again) carries the full force of nature reclaiming the very infrastructure of imperial Rome as if it were reverting to its original state of grass and bare hill, with which the *silva* begins.

Remains of the triumphal arches and gates show the collapse of empire more powerfully than does any other structure within this devastated urban landscape. The gates have toppled into uneven, asymmetrical ruins ("ruinas desiguales," 74). Trophies and blazons inscribed on arches are buried in the Tiber. The river, which had served to mirror their beauty, is now a tomb that weeps for them: "que el Tibre, que fue espejo a su hermosura, / los da en sus ondas llanto y sepultura" (1:264.70–1), an image presaged by the arches of its collapsed bridges, eyes "crying" its currents.

There are echoes in these lines of Quevedo's sonnet "A Roma sepultada en sus ruinas" (To Rome buried in its ruins), which like the *silva* is indebted to the European poetry of ruins and is addressed to a pilgrim. The lyric voice starts with a phrase made famous by an epigram of the neo-Latin poet Janus Vitalis in his *Roma prisca*, which is imitated by du Bellay in his *Antiquitez*, among others: "Buscas en Roma a Roma, ¡oh, peregrino! / y en Roma misma a Roma no la hallas" (You search for Rome in Rome, oh pilgrim, / and in Rome itself you do not find Rome).[11] Privileging the Tiber as a tomb, its waters weep over its lost city:

> Sólo el Tibre quedó, cuya corriente,
> si ciudad la regó, ya, sepoltura,
> la llora con funesto son doliente. (1:418)
>
> (Only the Tiber remains, whose current once
> watered the city; now a tomb, it weeps
> for her in painful, funeral dirge.)

Body Fragments

Equally evocative within Rome's landscape of ruins are the broken statues, which the *silva* stages through an allusion to Ovid's myth of Deucalion and Pyrrha. To regenerate the human race, which perished after

Jupiter unleashed a flood, the couple throw stones over their shoulders. These take on human form (*Metamorphoses* 1:401–15). Quevedo writes:

las peñas que vivieron
dura vida, con almas imitadas,
que parece que fueron
por Deucalión tiradas,
no de ingeniosa mano adelgazadas,
son troncos lastimosos,
robados sin piedad de los curiosos. (1.264.86–92)

(the statues that lived
in hard stone, with imitated souls,
that seemed to have been
thrown by Deucalion,
not carved by an ingenious hand,
are now pitiful trunks,
robbed without pity by the curious.)

Imperial Rome's statues, given life by artists and seeming to bear "souls," like Deucalion's newly formed humans, are now broken stone, "lifeless" trunks deprived of heads and limbs gathered by passers-by, literally "the curious" (los curiosos). The narrator commiserates with the corporeal fragments that have fallen into strange hands, "robados sin piedad" (stolen without pity). Here the rhetoric of ruins blends with the culture of collectionism in a formulation of the humanist engagement with the material remains of ancient Rome, for the technical term *curiosos* points to private collectors who acquire all sorts of objects, including statuary, often for display in a Wunderkammer, their cabinets of curiosities.[12] From the beginning of the sixteenth century, Roman collectors placed their broken antiquities in gardens and in villa courtyards. Ulisse Aldrovandi recorded scenes of the Palazzo Medici-Madama, which housed many fragmented antiquities in a kind of graveyard of once "living" statues, eerie in their representation of gods and goddesses who once were "alive," at least in the ancient imagination: "There is a seated nude Venus, in a position of reclining downward, who seems to be covering herself in front with her hands, but she has neither hands nor head … There is another quite beautiful nude Bacchus, but he has no head or arms … There is a trunk with grapes and a serpent wound around it, and with that another smaller nude statue without head or arms, and missing one leg – all out of one piece of marble."[13] Maarten van Heemskerck, who visited Rome in the

Figure 2.3 Maarten van Heemskerck, *Garden Loggia at Palazzo Madama*, 1532–6, pen and brown ink, fol. 5 recto. From the Roman Sketchbook 1. Photograph: Jörg P. Anders. Kupferstichkabinett, Staatliche Museen, Berlin. Art Resource, New York.

mid-1500s, sketched many of these statues at the Madama, including broken marble figures resting against vaulted columns (fig. 2.3). As Leonard Barkan has observed, the private display of *spolia* allowed for a "fetishistic viewing" of mutilated bodies and the contemplation of fragments with a relic-like reverence. "The owners of the collection and in turn those who record it for posterity," writes Barkan, "display these mutilated works with no shame or apology, recognizing them as beautiful despite the carefully catalogued missing parts that under other circumstances might cause them to be considered monstrosities" (1999, 121). Like Quevedo's library, which created a discursive space for conversing with the dead through books (see chapter 1), a courtyard collection offered a space for contemplating Rome's past through its fractured antiquities. Yet for Quevedo, stolen fragments of statuary, proclaiming Rome as the city of the "dead," violated the memory of imperial Rome.

Textual Fragments

The plundering of sculptural fragments in the streets of Rome mirrors another type of plundering, that of texts, *spolia* that become the building blocks of Quevedo's poem of ruins. The double dynamic between materiality and poetics, between material culture and the active "dismembering" of texts and the "reconstruction" of their fragments in a new discursive space, is what gives "Roma antigua y moderna" its distinctive quality. Quevedo, like Petrarch, searches for vestiges of the past and feels nostalgia for its lost remnants, but in writing about ruins, he "plunders" the city's "scattered remains" to construct his new Rome, as does notably Joachim du Bellay. "Du Bellay frequently uses 'la poudreuse cendre' (the dusty ashes) in *Les Antiquitez de Rome*," writes Andrew Hui, "to imagine Rome as a human body lying in ruins. His poetic ambition is to transport its dislocated fragments to adorn the architecture of his own nation. For his lyric to emerge from the smoldering ashes of antiquity, he willed, dreamed, needed Rome to be in ruins, in order to create his new vernacular monument" (2016, 20). If Quevedo needed Rome's ruins to construct a "new vernacular monument," he also needed fragments of texts, du Bellay's in particular, to carry out his lyric enterprise for Spain. Rodrigo Cacho Casal, who has recently explored Quevedo's literary journey to Rome and its ruins, privileges du Bellay's *Antiquitez* and *Poemata*, along with works of other early moderns, like the neo-Latin poet Janus Vitalis, as models for Quevedo's baroque *silva*. For Quevedo, the past was encoded as much in the material as in the textual. Rome's ruins augured ill for the crumbling medieval walls of Madrid (2009, 1171, 1174–6).[14]

The Ruins of Madrid

Four years before his visit to Rome, Quevedo wrote a more personal meditation on ruins in his sonnet "Miré los muros de la patria mía," *salmo* 17 of his *Heráclito cristiano*, which I examine briefly to offer some suggestive relations on the common threads running through the *silva* and the sonnet. The sonnet reads:

Miré los muros de la patria mía,
si un tiempo fuertes, ya desmoronados,
de la carrera de la edad cansados,
por quien caduca ya su valentía.

Salime al campo, vi que el sol bebía
los arroyos del yelo desatados,
y del monte quejosos los ganados,
que con sombras hurtó su luz al día.
Entré en mi casa; vi que, amancillada,
de anciana habitación era despojos;
mi báculo, más corvo y menos fuerte;
vencida de la edad sentí mi espada.
Y no hallé cosa en que poner los ojos
que no fuese recuerdo de la muerte. (1:184–5)

(I gazed upon my country's walls,
once strong, but crumbling now;
worn out by the race of years,
which has wasted all their strength.
I went out into the fields, I saw the sun
drinking the brooks, now freed from winter's ice,
and cattle moaning in the mountain,
as the light of day was overrun by shadows.
I went into my house; I saw my room
old and worn, now all rubble;
my cane less strong and bent;
I saw my sword overcome with age,
and there was not a thing left on which to fix my gaze
that was not a reminder of death.)[15]

Conceived as a recollection, Quevedo's meditation does not identify the walls by name, the "muros desmoronados," an omission that has given way to much speculation. I argue that Quevedo may be referring to Madrid's Muslim and Christian medieval walls (built by Abd al-Rahman III in 912–61, and reinforced and extended by Alfonso VII in the twelfth century). The Flemish artist Anton van den Wyngaerde's watercolour of 1564 show some of these walls still standing, though the towers show some decay (fig. 2.4). But by the turn of the seventeenth century, as attested by Jerónimo de Quintana in his 1629 chronicle (facsimile edition, 1980), these walls, with their gates and towers, were crumbling, some had disappeared, and others were being dismantled altogether for urban renewal (as had been the case with Rome's imperial architecture).[16] A witness to the devastation that was taking place before his eyes, Quintana writes alarmingly of the Christian walls, bemoaning their loss, aware that cultural memory and a country's heritage reside in these material remains:

> Esta cerca, como menos antigua que la primera, aunque lo es harto, está más en pie, y se ve más potente; si bien está desmantelada por algunas partes, y cada vez la van derribando por hartas; cosa que debiera conservarse, y no dar lugar a que se perdieran memorias de tanta importancia [...] pues por eso [los pueblos] vienen a perder la noticia de su antigüedad. (Cited in Gea Ortigas and Castellanos Oñate 2008, 140)
>
> (Since this wall is less ancient than the first [the Muslim wall], even if it is itself quite old, it is on better footing and looks stronger; although it has collapsed in several areas, and more and more it is being dismantled; a wall that should be preserved, so that memories of such importance are not lost ... since that is how countries lose knowledge of their ancient heritage.)

Like Rome's ruins, representing for Quevedo the fall of empire, Madrid's decayed walls inspire a silent political commentary, occasioned by the impoverishment and decadence of Spain under Philip III. The term *valentía* perhaps points surreptitiously to Spain's loss of the courage and fortitude that had sustained Habsburg Spain in the past. Vulnerable and not able to criticize the king and his *valido* openly, Quevedo mentions the corrosive passing of time as a cause of ruination, unlike Quintana's pointed critique of the dismantling of the old walls of Madrid.

If the sonnet and the *silva* share the notion of political and social collapse, which the lyric speaker projects onto the architectural ruins of Rome and Madrid, in the sonnet, however, the feelings of nostalgia are more intense as another Baroque theme enters the text, a blurring of the porous boundaries between the self and its surroundings, of inner and external landscapes. The lyric speaker projects his spiritual impoverishment and the devastating effects of the passage of time on his room and its objects – his melancholia embedded in his bent cane, a symbol of old age; and the old sword, remembrance of a heroic past and codes of honour, now lost. Death pervades the sonnet as household objects become profound reminders: "Y no hallé, *cosa* en que poner los ojos / que no fuera recuerdo de la muerte" (and there was not a *thing* left on which to fix my gaze / that was not a reminder of death; my emphasis). In the *silva*, too, the architectural remains are reminders of death, most vividly as collapsed into the Tiber, conceived as a tomb.[17]

The Capitoline Museum

"Roma antigua y moderna" is more than a poem of ruins. The narrator turns from his litany of destruction and decay to address Rome, which he had earlier personified as "Roma generosa" (line 64), praising her

Figure 2.4 Anton van den Wyngaerde, *The Medieval Walls of Madrid*, 1564, brown ink, watercolour. Album / Art Resource, New York.

for having "saved" from ruination the prized artefacts that survive as authentic carriers of ancient Roman culture:

> *Sólo* en el Capitolio perdonaste
> las estatuas y bultos que hallaste,
> y fue, en tu condición, gran cortesía,
> bien que a tal majestad se le debía. (1:264.93–6; my emphasis)
>
> (*Only* in the Capitoline you pardoned
> the statues and busts you found;
> and there was, in your capacity, great courtesy,
> the kind which was owed to such majesty.)

There at the Capitoline, the political and religious epicentre of ancient Rome, the narrator views the equestrian statue of Marcus

Aurelius, the *Trophies of Marius*, and inscribed funerary urns. Awestruck by the spectacle, he drops his impersonal mask to become a first-person narrator:

Allí del arte *vi* el atrevimiento;
pues Marco Aurelio, en un caballo, armado,
el laurel en las sienes añudado,
osa pisar el viento,
y en delgado camino y sendas puras
hallan donde afirmar sus herraduras.
De Mario *vi*, y lloré, desconocida,
la estatua a su fortuna merecida;
vi en las piedras guardados
los reyes y los cónsules pasados;
vi los emperadores,
dueños del poco espacio que ocupaban,
donde *sólo* por señas acordaban
que donde sirven hoy fueron señores. (1.264–5.97–110; my emphasis)

(There *I saw* the audacity of art;
for Marcus Aurelius armed, on his horse,
the laurel knotted on his temples,
dares to ride the wind;
and on a narrow road and pure paths
the horseshoes find space on which to leave their imprint.
Of Marius *I saw*, and wept for
his statue, unknown, but merited by his fortune;
I saw preserved in stone
past kings and consuls;
I saw emperors,
masters of the little space they occupied,
remembered *only* by signs
that where they serve today, they once were lords.)

Why did the artefacts of the Capitoline so impress Quevedo, and how did he read them? Daniel Sherman and Irit Rogoff observe that "museums both sustain and construct cultural master narratives that achieve an internal unity by imposing one cultural tendency as the most prominent manifestation of any historical period." A museum establishes the context that "provides the object with meaning, but at the same time, the context works to determine the selection of viewing public and the cultural capital that this public gleans from the museum" (1994, xi–xii). Quevedo found the essence of ancient Rome, not in its cityscape of ruins but in the museum, in bronze and stone statuary, precisely because they were imbued with the "cultural capital" that he sought to recover.

What Quevedo saw, in fact, was an artfully crafted site of memory, a curated collection of artefacts presenting a master narrative of the past for public viewing and contemplation. If a museum shapes knowledge by imposing its privileged script on spectators, argues Charles Garoian, they challenge the script by bringing to it their own knowledge and narratives (2001, 237). Quevedo is, in Garoian's term, "performing the museum," as he engages in a dialogic exchange with the museum's collections.[18] For Quevedo, who was no ordinary pilgrim, but a visitor enriched with a splendid humanist learning, the Capitoline as a space of performance offered him an opportunity to dialogue directly with ancient Rome. If he does not challenge the script furnished by the first museum of antiquities of the early modern era, he does reframe it by imposing his personal memory and own sense of cultural history on its artefacts.

What most captured the visitor's attention was his face-to-face encounter with the gilded bronze equestrian statue of the Stoic emperor Marcus Aurelius (121–80 CE), which Pope Paul III had relocated from the Lateran to the Capitoline in 1537, and Michelangelo placed in the centre of the Piazza dei Campidoglio (fig. 2.5). He admires the daring of art ("del arte vi el atrevimiento") behind which stands the skill of the artist. The mounted emperor dares to ride the wind as his horse sets its hoofs on the narrowest of platforms – "osa pisar el viento, / y en delgado camino y sendas puras / hallan donde afirmar sus herraduras" (and on a narrow road and pure paths / its horseshoes find space on which to leave their imprint), a delicate imagery at once an act of "historical recuperation" and "aesthetic pleasure" that calls for a celebration of ancient craftsmanship. The statue had survived through the centuries because it was long identified with Emperor Constantine, but by Quevedo's time it carried an inscription placed by Pope Sixtus IV proclaiming its true identity for all to see. Quevedo, the viewer of this culturally charged space, declares his subjectivity through the *vi* (I saw), relating to the dead emperor as if to a human presence – "Marco Aurelio, en un caballo, armado" (Marcus Aurelius armed, on his horse) – in an act of praise and intimacy, not with the statue but with the emperor himself. No mention is made of the emperor's

Figure 2.5 *Equestrian Statue of Marcus Aurelius*, c. 161–80 CE, gilded bronze. Palazzo dei Conservatori, Musei Capitolini, Rome. © Vanni Archive/ Art Resource, New York

Stoicism, which for the neo-Stoic Quevedo – an enthusiastic reader of Seneca, Epictetus, and Justus Lipsius, and perhaps Marcus Aurelius's *Meditations* as well – surely must have factored in his enthusiastic response to the sculpture.[19]

If Marcus Aurelius appears not merely as a sculptural representation but as a living presence in his bodily splendour on the Capitoline, the *Trophies of Marius* (fig. 2.6) remain enigmatic in the absence of human figures. The two marble statues, probably commemorating a first-century victory under Emperor Domitian, were transferred to the Capitoline from a nymphaeum in the Esquiline in the 1590s. Each is a fifteen-foot-high display of the spoils of war – shields, armour, prisoners – piled up around the frame of a victorious warrior, whose body is missing. The identification of Marius – Roman general, consul, and politician from the time of the Republic – with the *Trophies* came from a description of his victory over the Germanic Cimbri in Plutarch and Suetonius (Barkan 1999, 135). Quevedo accepts the traditional identification, "la estatua a su fortuna merecida" (the statue merited by his fortune), the presence of a certain majesty, but is moved to weep openly for the absent body, the unknown statue ("estatua desconocida"). The *Trophies* as "human representations that are empty of the human," writes Barkan, are like the statues "that were once whole but are now missing body parts" (136), scattered throughout the Roman cityscape. In a fashion, ruins have entered the Capitoline.

The emperors who lie in funerary urns in this museum and are known only from the inscriptions ("señas") that memorialize them in a "typical graphic culture of death," are also closely connected to the bodily ruination perceived elsewhere in the city.[20] Masters only of the little space they occupy, their bodies are "clothed" by dust, their memory by oblivion:

y yacen, poco peso, en urnas frías,
y visten (¡ved la edad cuánto ha podido!)
sus huesos polvo, y su memoria, olvido. (1:265.120–2)

(and they languish, weighing little, in cold urns;
and they wear (see how much time has triumphed!)
their bones dust, and their memory, oblivion.)

But the text quickly recovers the glory that was Rome by tracing its rebirth through a series of military and political events. The narrator passes from the siege of Rome by the Gauls (390 BCE), when Marcus

Figure 2.6 *Trophies of Marius*. Master of the Oxford Album, folios 37, 62, recto. Campidoglio balustrade, Rome. © Ashmolean Museum, University of Oxford.

Figure 2.6 (Continued)

Manlius, awakened by the squawking of the sacred geese, repelled the enemy besieging the Capitoline (1:265.126–30); to Crassus's quelling of Spartacus's revolt (71 BCE) (1.265.138–9); then to Nero's burning of Rome (64 CE) (1.265–6.141–6). Those events are cast as pivotal to Rome's rebirth as a phoenix: "pero de las cenizas que derramas / fénix renaces, parto de las llamas, / haciendo tu fortuna / tu muerte vida y tu sepulcro cuna" (1.266.147–50; you are reborn from the flames and ashes as a phoenix, and your fortune transforms your death into life, and your tomb into a cradle). The endpoint of the transformations of Rome is papal Rome in which the present faces the imperial past directly, free of any imprint by the intervening centuries.

The Papal Landscape

Quevedo ends the poem in his own time, in the now of papal Rome. The popes had played a highly active role in forming the political and cultural life of modern Rome, a role not addressed in the *silva* but critical to understanding how the popes altered the cityscape. The Capitoline statues were part of a carefully staged appropriation of Rome's past by popes who had been dedicated collectors of antiquities since the mid-fifteenth century. Communicating with ancient Rome's past was, for them, a means of legitimizing and extending their hold over the city. Sixtus IV (1471–84) began the urban renewal that eventually transformed Rome from a medieval to a Renaissance city. He rebuilt many of the old churches and chapels, established the Vatican library, encouraged the construction of palaces to replace medieval residences, and opened roads for pilgrims, to make Rome, in effect, a new Jerusalem. In 1471 he sent several bronze sculptures, which had been on display in front of the papal palace at the Lateran (including the *Spinario,* the *Lupa,* and fragments of the colossus of Constantine), to the Conservators' Palace on the Capitoline Hill, where they became the core collection of the museum (Christian 2010, 92, 104; Benzi 2000). As he proclaimed in a commemorative plaque, his gifts "returned" to the Roman people, the *popolo romano,* the "testaments of Rome's ancient virtue and surpassing achievement" (Stinger 1998, 256). But the pope's gift was also a scheme of appropriation designed to establish a papal presence and authority on the Capitoline through Rome's antiquities, and to create a symbolic bridge between the former centre of imperial Rome and modern papal Rome, legitimizing the papacy as ancient Rome's true heir.

Figure 2.7 Étienne Dupérac (1535–1604), *Etching after Michelangelo's Design for the Capitol Square in Rome*. Erich Lessing/Art Resource, New York.

In the mid-sixteenth century, Pope Paul III (1534–49) extended Sixtus's political agenda. He famously demolished both ancient and medieval buildings to make way for Charles V's triumphal entry into Rome in 1536, after his victory at the Battle of Tunis; the triumphal route, designed to pass through the city, ended at Saint Peter's Basilica, where the pope welcomed the emperor. Two years later Paul commissioned Michelangelo to redesign the Capitoline, to reorient it to face the basilica, away from the Forum, in a sense to turn its back on the centre of ancient Rome's public life (fig. 2.7). The Capitoline, the Senators Palace, the spectacular statue of Marcus Aurelius, the set of stairs leading to the piazza and flanked by the balustrade with the statues of the Dioscuri (Castor and Pollux), and the *Trophies of Marius* – all looked straight ahead to Saint Peter's, while Saint Peter's, reciprocally, extended its own aura over the Capitoline.

At the end of "Roma antigua y moderna," the third-person narrator emerges as a commentator and advocate of papal Rome. Siding with the Santos Pontífices, he leaves behind the ruins and Capitoline antiquities to reframe Rome and the papal mastery of the city by addressing a different set of objects endowed with symbolic value:

Las águilas trocaste por la llave,
y el nombre de ciudad por el de Nave:
los que fueron Nerones insolentes,
son Píos y Clementes. (1.266.171–4)

(The eagles you traded for the key
and the name of city for that of Ship:
those who once were insolent Neros
are now Piuses and Clements.)

The imperial eagle gives way to the key of Saint Peter, the first pope, and the city is re-imagined as the "Nave," figuratively the Ship of the faithful and concretely the nave of Saint Peter's Basilica built over Peter's tomb. Christian architecture has replaced and superseded imperial Rome's. The poem's last two lines, alluding to the current religious and political wars, sum up Quevedo's turn to Catholic Rome in its non-material guise: "tú [Roma] [...] / en tan dura guerra, / gloriosa corte de la fe en la tierra" (1.266, 179–80; you, in such harsh war, the glorious court of faith on earth). Pulled back from Rome's past, he praises its present rulers, the Piuses and Clements, and their new Christian values. The poem ends abruptly, not as in a traditional poem of ruins but firmly relocated in a new Rome. The *huésped* reveals himself as a pilgrim in a religious sense. His wandering is redefined as a pilgrimage to a sacred space; and the temporal shifting of "then" and "now" ends within an atemporal city of the popes ("corte de la fe en la tierra"), in a sense a city of God on earth.

Chapter Three

Producing Pastoral Spaces

Luis de Góngora (1561–1627) was *docto* like Francisco de Quevedo, but with a daring, exuberant complexity and ornamentation that earned him entry into the *secta de los culteranos*, so called by its detractors for its outlandish style, a sect that was to them a heresy (*luterano*, echoing in *culterano*). Like Quevedo, Góngora shares fully in the poetics of the material, most memorably in his sonnet epitaph to the marble tomb of El Greco; in his celebration of the towers and walls of his native Córdoba and the secular and religious buildings of Toledo; his figuration of woman's body through jewels, precious stones, and metal; in his extravagant display of the material riches, especially diamonds and paintings, in the *camarín* of poet aristocrat the Count of Villamediana.[1] Yet his most complex and subtle exploration of the material, save perhaps for his *Soledades*, is his pastoral *Fábula de Polifemo y Galatea* (1613), a reworking of the ancient myth, mapped and orchestrated within a set of spatial frames, interactive landscapes replete with objects, where even time and sonority are materialized.

My reading relies on two related insights: Michel de Certeau's notion of space as a practised place, here understood as a physical site transformed by social and cultural activities;[2] and W.J.T Mitchell's view of landscape as "a natural scene mediated by culture," a medium of exchange and a site for "visual appropriation" and the formation of identity ([1994] 2002). I ask where and how a physical *place* becomes a social *space* in *Polifemo*'s landscapes: in the Count of Niebla's Andalusian estate; in Polyphemus's cave on an ash-covered plain and a rock on a Sicilian promontory; in the *locus amoenus* of Acis and Galatea; and in the liminal space of the seashore. How are identities constructed within those interactive scenes, filled with objects? How does vision become a dynamic force in mediating personal relationships and validating identities? How does sonority contribute to the production of space, and how does time enact its own material performance as it moves from dawn to midday to dusk, traversing the spaces of the count, the giant, and the lovers?

Within those mobile spaces, Góngora practises his baroque craft, creating a rhetoric of the object or, better yet, a poetics of objects made luminous and beautiful. In the words of Octavio Paz, "el mundo de Góngora es un espacio henchido de colores, formas, individuos y objetos particulares [...] En Góngora triunfa la luz: todo, hasta la tiniebla, resplandece [...] La tentativa poética de Góngora consiste en substituir la realidad que vemos por otra, ideal" (1982, 470). (The world of Góngora is a space full of colours, forms, individuals and particular objects ... In Góngora light triumphs: everything, even darkness, shines ... Góngora's poetic objective consists in substituting the reality that we see for an ideal reality.)

The poem opens with a scene of cultural production, in which writing is conceived in aural terms inspired by the pastoral yet learned muse Talía:

Estas que me dictó rimas sonoras,
culta sí, aunque bucólica, Talía
– *¡oh excelso conde!* – , en las purpúreas horas
que es rosas la alba y rosicler el día,
ahora que de luz tu Niebla doras,
escucha, al son de la zampoña mía,
si ya los muros no te ven, de Huelva,
peinar el viento, fatigar la selva. (1.1–8; my emphasis)[3]

(*These resonant rhymes that were dictated*
to me by the learned, yet bucolic, Thalia
– O exalted Count! – during the purple hours
when the dawn is roses and the day is deep red,
now that you are gilding your Niebla with light,
listen to them, sung to the sound of my pipes,
unless the walls of Huelva are now seeing you,
combing the wind, beating the forest, for game.)

The Latinism *dictar*, meaning both to inspire and to dictate, enacts a system of verbal signs that constructs the discursive space of Thalia and the poet, a space for singing and listening, and implicitly a space for reading. The muse Thalia is the source of song (of *poiesis*), which the poet as teller activates in performance for the count: "escucha, al son de la zampoña mía" (listen to them, sung to the sound of my pipes).

Chromatic hues share in the production of space. Materialized as roses, dawn activates the landscape with its sparkling colours, purple and deep red, setting the stage for the muse to inspire and "dictate" her "sonorous rhymes." This is an instance of the poetics of light that Robert Hudson Vincent has recently claimed for the *Polifemo*, placing silently Octavio Paz's hyperbolic "light triumphs ... everything, even darkness, shines" within the context of Johannes Kepler's theories of optics, which makes light the agent of vision, with colour a significant aspect of refraction (Vincent 2018, 231–32).[4] In the light-drenched space of storytelling at the beginning of the *Polifemo*, Thalia's name resonates – its etymology pointing to the muse as one who "flourishes," who "brings flowers," who enables "growth and blooming." As an emblem of a poetry of excess, the muse is located within the shimmering luxurious setting of a Homeric dawn, the time of day that, as the ancients proclaimed, is a time of creativity and inspiration.

The Count's Domain

The count shares in the poetics of light and colour as he enters the village of Niebla, his Andalusian estate, "gilding" it by imprinting it with his presence, his aura, like a sun bathing with its rays the mist (a play on the Spanish word *niebla*). At that moment, however, the text announces that he may be in the forest near Huelva, hunting with his falcons and for small game, the sports of kings and nobles, where he acts out his aristocratic status, thus transforming the forest into a relational, practised place. The city of Huelva, taking on life, participates in his performance: its walls, endowed with eyes, are complicit in his figuration, validating his status as hunter and count.

Entreating the count to quiet the animals of the hunt for the storytelling (stanza 2), the narrative voice dwells on their refined accessories, signalling his aristocratic identity (2.9–16): let the falcon on its perch try to deny his *bell* ("desmentir al *cascabel* presuma"); let the vibrant Andalusian horse stand still, coating its *golden bit* with white, idle foam ("tascando haga el *freno de oro*, cano, [...] la ociosa espuma"); let the hound pine on its *silken leash* ("gima el lebrel en *el cordón de seda*"); let the hunter's horn ("el cuerno") be silenced and replaced by the zither ("la cítara"), the polished instrument of poetry. The bell, the golden bit, the silken leash, and the horn all belong to the count's space, which envelopes and characterizes him. And here as in the *Soledades*, where Góngora "entreats the duke to relinquish his temporal power and concede supremacy and leadership to the poet in the space of the imagination"

(Collins 2002, 9), the count would put aside his aristocratic objects and would enter the poet's discursive space in gentle silence ("dulce silencio") and attentive ease ("ocio atento") – *ocio* typically calling attention to this space as one of leisure and creativity – so as to listen to the fierce song of the musical giant ("del músico jayán el fiero canto"; 3.17–19) under a stately canopy ("dosel augusto") erected in the forest, as if at court in the wild. Poet and patron, teller and audience, and silence and sonority interact to produce a cultured text befitting its aristocratic recipient. In juxtaposing Thalia's dictation with the count's hunting, two cultural practices that transform place into space, Góngora draws our attention to a dynamic that will define the spaces of his poem.

The narrator begins with memorably sonorous lines: "Donde espumoso el mar sicilïano / el pie argenta de plata al Lilibeo" (4.25–6; Where the rich foam of the Sicilian sea plates with silver the foot of Lilibaeum). The Lilibaeum, a promontory on the westernmost part of Sicily, overlooks the Mediterranean shore. Why does the poet signal the seashore, a luminous space between sea and land, at the very start of the storytelling? In *Cinematic Overtures: How to Read Opening Scenes* (2017), Annette Insdorf may give a clue. She writes: "First impressions count. A strong opening sequence leads the spectator to trust the filmmakers" (ix). "My experience watching films," she continues, "suggests that a great movie tends to provide in the first few minutes the keys by which to unlock the rest of the film." Here, too, first impressions count and provide keys to highlight the poem's style and unlock significant scenes. The strikingly visual "argenta de plata," literally to "silver-plate with silver," announces a grammar of images that alerts the reader not only to the gilding that defines Góngora's baroque style but also to the shore as a liminal space of performance through which all the actors, the walkers, pass: where Galatea leaves her footprint on the sand, and her suitors offer their gifts; where Polyphemus, sitting on a rock nearby, invites Galatea to join him and later sees his reflection in his mirror of sapphire ("espejo de zafiro"); where a shipwrecked Genoese is washed ashore with riches of the Orient; and where at the end of the tale, Acis, transformed into a river deity, "silvers" the sands with his waters, in a sense silvering what already had been silvered.

The Cave of Polyphemus

Polyphemus's cave appears on an ash-covered plain near the Lilibaeum where, as legend has it, deep within lie the subterranean forge of Vulcan – the god of fire and metalworking – and the tomb harbouring the bones of the serpentine monster Typhon, who even now spews fire and burning ash (4.25–9). This is a site of sacrilege, where Typhon, the son of Gaia and Tartarus, rebels against the gods (Ovid 1984, 1:5.321ff). Struck by Jupiter's thunderbolt (1:3.303), he is buried under Sicily (1:5.346–8). Those dark, violent presences precede Polyphemus in the dark landscape of volcanic eruptions, where his cave, barbaric and huge, is a realm of night "caliginoso lecho, el seno obscuro / ser de la negra noche" (5.37–8; in this dark refuge black night has her tenebrous couch). Sad and sombre nocturnal birds circle within ("infame turba de nocturnas aves, / gimiendo tristes y volando graves; 5.39–40), as if activating with their "moaning cries" that dark, ominous place, transforming it into a space of melancholy. The cave, a "huge yawn" of a personified earth ("formidable de la tierra / bostezo, el melancólico vacío"; 6.41–2), is emblematic of the Cyclops as a primeval being of Saturnine temperament, a sad and nostalgic creature of the night, his black hair dark as the waters of Hades's Lethe (8.57–8). His characteristic colour flows from black bile, one of the four bodily fluids associated with the melancholic temperament, as Galenic humoral theory prescribes. Significantly, the monster's melancholia is not described, only inferred from his dwelling and the "moaning" nocturnal birds hovering within. Like Kronberg Castle, its stones, walls, and courtyard absorbing Hamlet's dark aura and speaking his "language," which resonates in the visitors' memory (see introduction), Polyphemus's cave speaks his language as it absorbs his sombre, tenebrous persona.[5]

Crude and solitary, this self-sufficient goatherd is as much a creator of his space as a product of it. His identity is projected onto the domestic objects that he manufactures for his everyday living: his cane, his clothes, his bag, and his pipes. He shapes his cane from the highest pine in the mountain, bending it under his enormous weight as it turns from a "prop" to a "crook" for tending his goats (7.54–7). He makes his garment ("pellico") from the skin of the savage animals he kills (9.69–70). He crafts pipes from a hundred hollow canes that he binds with wax and hemp to summon a savage music, as barbaric as his cave ("bárbaro rüído"; 12.90). And he gathers fruit of the forest in a bag ("zurrón") that projects most authentically his formidable, monstrous self, couched in a baroque material discourse that encapsulates the process of producing space while constructing identity in a language of violent yet beautiful things. His bag is like a walled orchard, wide and stuffed with fruit, "Cercado es (cuanto más capaz, mas lleno) / de la fruta, el zurrón, casi abortada" (10.73–4). Huge and fertile, with the fruit almost bursting out of its enclosure ("casi abortada"), the bag is almost unnatural, a compressed space tearing, almost spilling out in its overabundance. Like Polyphemus's enormous body, a virtual mountain of a landscape ("un monte era de miembros eminente"; 7.49), the fruit bag bears its own crushing violence within. The barbarous sound of his pipes announces that same imminent violence to the undoing of the surrounding landscape, which becomes an ominous soundscape: the uproar of the forests, the storms at sea, the fleeing ships, and Triton, who breaks his twisted conch (12.93–5). The dark space of Polyphemus portends the poem's ending, when his contained violence explodes in anger and he kills Acis with a boulder snatched from his coarse landscape.

"Casi abortada" also points to the excesses of the baroque. Within this overabundance a point of light focuses on a telling luminous material presence that stands for Góngora's favorite aesthetic technique:

la pera, de quien fue cuna dorada
la rubia paja, y – pálida tutora –
la niega avara, y pródiga la dora. (10.78–80)

(the pear, whose golden cradle
was the blond straw, which – as a pale tutor –
closely guards and richly gilds.)

Pedro Salinas, writing on Góngora's "passion for the substance of material reality," notes that the poet "is enamoured of the real. But he exalts it, ennobles it in such a way that the world becomes a marvelous feast for the imagination and the senses" ([1966] 1980, 146).[6] The poet "gilds" the pear, which is lying on its golden straw cradle as it ripens in the fruit bag, as if he were describing a still life, rehearsing in this brief moment a contemporary pictorial code, the superseding of art over nature.[7] Like the gilding of Niebla by the Count's golden light and of the seashore by the sea, the gilding of the pear draws attention to Góngora's baroque craft, by which nature is reified and transformed into objects more perfect than nature's own.

If the bag, bursting with inner tensions, is a sign of its dark owner, so is the pear in its luminosity, for the text announces the Cyclops as a luminous figure of sorts: his eye, singled out by the narrator as shining *almost* like the sun ("émulo casi del mayor lucero"; 7.51–2), aligns him with light, with what Octavio Paz has detected in the play of light and darkness in the *Polifemo*, "hasta la tiniebla, resplandece" (1982, 470; everything, even darkness, shines). Polyphemus is in effect a "black sun," Julia Kristeva's term for a simultaneously dark and luminous melancholy figure. In her study of depression and melancholia Kristeva examines this figure in Gerard de Nerval's sonnet "El Desdichado" in ways that are suggestive here. The first quatrain reads:

> Je suis le ténébreux, – le veuf, – l'inconsolé,
> Le prince d'Aquitaine à la tour abolie;
> Ma seule *étoile* est morte, – et mon luth constellé
> Porte le *Soleil noir* de la *Mélancolie*.
>
> (I am saturnine – bereft – disconsolate,
> The Prince of Aquitaine whose tower has crumbled;
> My lone star is dead – and my bespangled lute
> Bears the *Black Sun* of Melancholia.)
>
> (Kristeva 1989, 141; emphasis in the original)

Kristeva connects "ténébreux" ("dark," thus "saturnine") with the Prince of Darkness and as such with Pluto, "whose deformity caused the goddesses to flee" (1989, 146). She also connects the term with "night deprived of light," conjuring up "the melancholy person's complicity with the world of darkness and despair" (147). For Kristeva, the "black sun" "takes up the semantic field of 'saturnine'" but turns it "inside out, like a glove: darkness flashes as a solar light, which nevertheless remains dazzling with black invisibility" (147). The darkness of the melancholy mood belongs to the "celestial realm" (151) and, as such, flairs out like a dazzling sun, blinding in its power. So, it is with Polyphemus's own darkness, its source a complex mix of monstrous violence and melancholia. His eye, which the narrator defines as almost like a sun, and, as we will see, the Cyclops deems a sun, is the very sign of his monstrosity. As it flashes its brilliance, it flashes its monstrous darkness, a deformity that, like Pluto's, causes his own goddess to flee.

Galatea's Space

Leaving the dark world of the Cyclops, the narrative shifts to Galatea's luminous space. In Ovid's version of the tale, in *Metamorphoses* 13 (1984, 738–897), the foundational text and master narrative for Góngora, Galatea has voice, as she tells her story to fellow sea-nymphs, the Nereids, who gather around her.[8] In the *Polifemo*, she is stripped of voice. Reduced to a splendid prop without agency, she becomes a seductive spectacle for the eyes of her suitors (Friedman 1995, 70). All light and delicate beauty, befitting her origin in the "kingdom of foam" (el reino de la espuma; 13.98), she is an elusive, ethereal figure, a type of Venus, whose body lies hidden through catachresis (an intensified metaphor lacking a primary term): her radiant and translucent skin is projected materially as Neptune's "crystal rock" (13.103), and as "white feather" on which her luminous eyes shine (13.102).[9] The eyes of the sea – like the eyes of Huelva's walls, which validate the count's figuration – confirm her beauty: "Ninfa, de Doris hija, la más bella, / adora, *que vio el reino de la espuma*" ([Polifemo] adores a nymph, Doris's daughter, fairer than any the waves' kingdom has ever seen; 13.97–8, my emphasis).

Galatea's space is one of transformation. Dawn and Cupid, silently and theatrically, dress her for her performance as an object of desire and contemplation, carried out by an act of layering, a technique used throughout to enhance her beauty. Showering deep-red rose petals over her white lilies (her white skin), Dawn creates a perfectly coloured complexion, "púrpura nevada, o nieve roja" (14.108; snowy red or red snow). Cupid, acting as a goldsmith, does one better, gilding her in an overlay by taking from the Red Sea a pearl ("perla Eritrea"), whose whiteness competes with Galatea's brow; encasing it in gold, he places it on her ear, conceived through catachresis as a seashell ("condenando su esplendor, la deja / pender en *oro* al *nácar* de su oreja"; 14.111–12, my emphasis).[10] Adorned in pearls, Galatea conforms to the contemporary fashion of aristocratic ladies depicted in paintings of the period, who were outfitted in jewelled dresses, with strings of pearls in their hair, and adorned with pearl necklaces, pendants, and earrings. A portrait of Queen Margaret of Austria shows her wearing pearl earrings and a large pendant with three pearls on her bodice (fig. 3.1). Bartolomé González, a follower of court portraitist Juan Pantoja de la Cruz, painted her wearing a matching pearl tiara (fig. 3.2).

Bejewelled Galatea, hiding behind veils of luxury and appearing ethereal and elusive, enigmatic and ultimately invisible, stands better than any other character in the *Polifemo* for the baroque aesthetic of objects. In *The Writing of History* Michel de Certeau says of the baroque: "[it] is a spectacle of metamorphoses which ceaselessly hide what they show … [A] shimmering of appearances speaks for the inaccessibility of the 'real'" (1988, 145n33). We may ask of Galatea's baroque performance, in her own spectacle of transformation, what is it that she hides and what is it that she shows, and to what purpose? We are shown stones and pearls, luxurious materials veiling her body, but not her body itself. Materiality resides in her signs. Paul Julian Smith comments on the woman's

Figure 3.1 School of Frans Pourbus the Younger, *Portrait of Margaret of Austria, Queen of Spain (1584–1611)*. Private Collection. HIP/Art Resource, New York.

Figure 3.2 Bartolomé González, *Queen Margaret of Austria*, 1609, oil on canvas. Museo del Prado, Madrid. © Museo Nacional del Prado./Art Resource, New York.

body and its invisibility in the *Polifemo* in words that echo de Certeau. Mediated through catachresis, her body is always distanced, always at "one remove, in an indefinite suspension" (1989, 63). Smith offers an example, the image of Galatea's limbs as jasmines: "tantos jazmines cuanta hierba esconde / la nieve de sus miembros" (23.179–80; as many jasmines as the grass hidden by the snow of her limbs), "emblematic of a shimmering linguistic surface which refuses to be anchored safely to the solid materiality of a pre-existing referent" (Smith 1989, 64). If Galatea's body is inaccessible in this metaphoric surface, anchored not on the materiality of her body but on the materiality of luxury objects and things of nature, then a shimmering that "speaks for the inaccessibility of the 'real'" follows Galatea from place to place, imbuing each with her evanescent aura.

The elusive Galatea fleeing her suitors on land and sea is conveyed in images fittingly centred on her foot – a fetish typically part of a collection of corporeal objects in the tradition of the anatomical blason. Here, however, the foot is conceived through movement while sea gods woo her in brief scenes of seduction. Glaucus bids her *to step on his crystal chariot* to cruise the silver waves: "*a pisar* [...] / *en carro de cristal*, campos de plata" (15.119–20; my emphasis). Palaemon follows her, swimming on the "foamy" sea, but she escapes as if bearing wings on her feet, *stepping on flowers* close to shore: "calzada plumas, / *tantas flores pisó* como él espumas" (16.27–8; my emphasis). The very place where *her foot stops* on the seashore – "que el margen *donde para* / del espumoso mar *su pie ligero*" (20.153–4, my emphasis; on the margin of the foamy sea, *where her agile foot stops*) – becomes an "altar," transformed by her Sicilian suitors into a space of pilgrimage, idolatry, and worship. In ritual gifting, the farmer offers his first crops, the shepherd his shearing, and the fruit grower a cornucopia of produce in a wicker basket woven by his chaste daughter: "de la Copia [...] el cuerno vierte el hortelano, entero, / sobre la mimbre que tejió, prolija, [...] su honesta hija" (20.157–60; the entire horn of plenty the fruit grower pours on the wicker woven slowly by his chaste daughter). Gifts – wheat, sheep's wool, and wine – are described through catachresis, "granos de oro" (grains of gold), "copos de nieve" (snowflakes), and "exprimida grana" (pressed-out purple) (19.147–50), a trope already owned by Galatea, the gifts' descriptors properly mirroring the recipient in their beauty.

A Space of Courtship

Abandoning her suitors, Galatea enters a *locus amoenus*, with its typical attributes of trees, shade, bird-song, water, a breeze, and flowers. It is midday, the time of pastoral, announced materially through the performance of a personified laurel hiding its trunk and foliage from the burning sun, implicitly producing the shade requisite to a *locus amoenus*: "hurta un laurel su tronco al sol ardiente" (23.178). In his classic definition of the traditional pastoral landscape, E.R. Curtius writes of it as a formulaic, earthly paradise, an artificial site, whose function is primarily rhetorical (1963, 192, 195–8). Yet in the *Polifemo* the *locus amoenus* is a dynamic space, one that functions according to what W.J.T. Mitchell asks of landscape, not just "what it 'is' or 'means,' but what it *does*, how it works as a cultural practice." "Like language or paint," Mitchell writes, "[it is] a body of symbolic forms capable of being invoked and reshaped" ([1994] 2002, 1, 14; emphasis in the original). His words resonate in Góngora's baroque space: "landscape is itself a physical and multisensory medium (earth, stone, vegetation, water, sky, sound and silence, light and darkness) in which cultural meanings and values are encoded, whether they are *put* there by the physical transformation of a place in landscape gardening and architecture [by artifice], or *found* in a place formed, as we say, 'by nature'" (14). Artifice first enters the landscape with Galatea. As she walks into the *locus amoenus*, her body merges with nature, magnifying its physical beauty by her white limbs, conceived through catachresis as jasmines, one of nature's most delicate of flowers, which cover the grass on which she lies next to the fountain, "tantos jazmines cuanta hierba esconde / la nieve de sus miembros, da a una fuente" (23.179–80; [she] yields to a spring as many jasmines as grass is hidden by the snow of her limbs). Through the artifice of rhetorical language, her body *becomes* landscape.

The landscape also becomes a soundscape, produced by two nightingales cooing in counterpoint – "Dulce se queja, dulce le responde / un ruiseñor a otro" (23.181–2; sweetly complains and sweetly responds one nightingale to another) – announcing the *locus amoenus* as an intimate retreat for the lovers' erotic encounter. Soon after, artifice re-enters the landscape in another guise: the lovers are cultural objects that leave their mark, their signature, on the landscape, transforming it. Acis, all dust and sweat in the midsummer heat, with beads of perspiration codified through catechresis as "aljófares," an Arabic neologism meaning "pearls" (24.188), eroticizes Galatea's idyllic space. With his entrance, the *locus amoenus* becomes a dynamic space of courtship through visual and erotic exchange and gift-giving. Looking at Galatea out of the corner of his eye while drinking from the fountain waters, Acis enters a world of visual enticement, of woman as erotic spectacle, her luminous quiet body depicted through catachresis as "silent crystal" (echoing Neptune's "crystal rock"), a material overlay that reinforces her compelling presence: "su boca dio, y sus ojos cuanto pudo, / al sonoro cristal, al cristal mudo" (24.191–2; he fastened his mouth to the sounding crystal stream and eyes, where he could, to the silent crystal). Laura Mulvey observes that "in their traditional exhibitionist role women are simultaneously looked at and displayed, with their appearance coded for strong visual and erotic impact … [S]he holds the look, plays to and signifies male desire" (1989, 19). As a magnet to steel and an idol to adoration, so her body draws his eyes: "El bello imán, el ídolo dormido, / que acero sigue, idólatra venera" (25.197–8). A breeze – materially conceived as delicate curtains drawn by the god of the wind – gently blowing over the nymph, who is lying on the grass, becomes delicately complicit in the act of exposing her body:

> Vagas cortinas de volantes vanos
> corrió Favonio lisonjeramente
> a la (de viento cuando no sea) cama
> de frescas sombras, de menuda grama. (27.213–16)

> (Drifting curtains, fleeting airy veils
> the breeze drew caressingly around her bed,
> an airy hammock not of knotted cord
> but of cool shade and fine grass.)

Awakened by the sound of the fountain waters, Galatea finds Acis's gifts beside her. Like her suitors' offerings at the seashore, his gifts are products of the land, though more alluring and strategically placed on finely crafted objects denoting the delicacy of the sophisticated seducer: a honeycomb in a small but skilfully shaped cork ("en breve corcho, pero bien labrado"), almonds on white wicker, and butter on green reeds (26.201–8). Here gift-giving creates an intimate personal bond. As Marcel Mauss writes, a gift bears the "soul" or "spirit" of the giver, the *hau* in Maori gift rituals. "To make a gift of something to someone," writes Mauss, "is to make a present of some part of one-self" (1990, 2). And if Mauss's theoretical formulation is correct – the gift, seemingly gratuitous, calls for a return – Galatea's body is to be that return.[11] As she awakens, in fear and startled by Acis's presence, she is portrayed as a frozen statue ("estatua helada"; 29.231).[12] While examining Acis's gifts, she is struck in the chest, conceived as a "crystal quiver" (carcaj de cristal; 31.243–4), by Cupid's gold dart, and her eyes awaken – "*mira* la ofrenda ya con más cuidado" (31.246; my emphasis) – to become active agents in her love adventure. Cupid's dart, acting as "a gentle brush," sketches her unnamed gift giver in her visual imagination, imprinted in an inner landscape as if on paper or canvas ("pincel süave / lo ha bosquejado ya en su *fantasía*" (32.251–2); my emphasis).

This passage is the product of a visual culture fascinated by the representation of interiority in material terms, as explained by theories of the imagination connected with optics. Drawing from a host of sources, from the ancients to Ficino to Freud, Giorgio Agamben identifies fantasy as the imaginative faculty that forms phantasms, mental images that create lasting impressions upon the soul. Images of objects are perceived by the senses and imagined as visions and in dreams (1993, 23). Cupid has imprinted Acis's image in Galatea's interior, a space for phantasms, echoing Plato's *Philebus* (Bergmann 1979, 249). For Socrates, the soul is conceived as a scriptable surface, a "book," where memory, sense perception, and the passions are transcribed by a "scribe," then illustrated by a "painter" (Plato 1993, 39a–b). Upon Galatea's awakening, her inner landscape is projected outward through vision, "full of color," revealing Acis in the flesh ("viendo colorido el bosquejo; 34.269–72). Reified and fetishized, his body merges with the natural landscape, as hers had earlier.

Del casi tramontado sol aspira
a los confusos rayos, su cabello:
flores su bozo es, cuyas colores,
como duerme la luz, niegan las flores. (35.277–80)

(His hair competes, like misty shafts of light,
with the sun about to set behind the mountain;
a shadow softly blooms on chin and lips
like flowers that hide their color when light sleeps.)

If Acis is all spectacle, Galatea is all eyes as she absorbs the love poison through his image (36.285–8), setting the stage for a visual exchange and appropriation. Acis, cast as Argus (the hundred-eyed creature, who is Juno's spy) returns her look through half-closed eyes.[13] His eroticized seeing is acute in vision and insight. If Acis, watching her every move, is an Argus, he is also a lynx, reading her every thought, breaching her inner space: "lince penetrador de lo que piensa, / cíñalo bronce o múrelo diamante" (37.293–4; a lynx to probe the thoughts that filled her mind, even were it shielded by bronze or walled by diamond).[14] Early modern theorists drew a direct connection between seeing and knowing. Emanuele Tesauro equates vision and cognition: "To look with the eyes and to contemplate with the intellect are two analogous types of knowledge" (cited in Quintero (2000, 492). Leon Battista Alberti goes one step further in *De pictura* (c. 1435), placing seeing and knowing in a relation of power. The geometrical analysis of the visual field in his theory of perspective, with its centrally fixed "vanishing point," yields epistemological mastery: "eye and knowledge come together; subject and object and the distance of the steady observation that allows the one to master the other" (Heath 1981, 30). Space theory calls attention to the centrality of power in human interaction. "Space thus produced," writes Henri Lefebvre, "also serves as a tool of thought and of action: that in addition to being a means of production it is also a means of control, and hence of domination, of power" ([1974] 1991, 26). Knowing Galatea's secret thoughts, Acis signals his mastery over her, in a prelude to possession.

In his delicate courtship, Acis attempts seduction: prostrated at her feet, white as ivory, he tries to kiss her golden sandals ("al marfil luego de sus pies rendido, / el coturno besar dorado intenta"; 38.299–300). Her feet had defined her elusiveness when she fled her suitors at the shore, but here she is anchored to Acis in a new space, a secluded spot where a hollow cliff provides a "shady canopy" (dosel umbroso; 39.310) and ivy protective "blinds" (verdes celosías; 39.311). Spring transforms nature into culture by "weaving" a carpet with silk more vibrant than Tyrian purple for the lovers' nuptial bed:[15]

Sobre una alfombra, que imitara en vano
el tirio sus matices (si bien era
de cuantas sedas ya hiló, gusano,
y, artífice, tejió la Primavera)
reclinados […] (40.313–17)

(They reclined upon a carpet whose hues the Tyrian
would imitate in vain (though it was made
by the silk spun by Spring as a worm and
woven by her as an artisan.)

M.J. Woods has called attention to nature's agency in the *Polifemo*. "It is interesting," he writes, "that Góngora should describe the perfection of his natural setting in terms appropriate to civilized life – carpets, canopies, blinds and four-poster beds … Góngora sees the beauty of nature as a kind of artifice, which means that he cannot be said to be seeking to establish an antithesis between the untamed natural world on the one hand, and the creations of artifice on the other" (1978, 156). Artifice is central to the baroque aesthetic of nature transformed into culture for the creation of beautiful objects. Voiceless and despite intimations of an inner life – the sketching of his figure in her imagination, her feelings as she hovers over him by turns agitated and hesitant, his reading of her thoughts – Acis and Galatea remain closed vessels in their visual silent loveliness, essentially bodies divested of interiority. Only Polyphemus is endowed with voice and subjectivity.

A Space of Melancholy

Dusk, materialized as the sun's horse chariot moving westward, announces a new landscape and a new soundscape, the violent world of Polyphemus:

Su aliento humo, sus relinchos fuego,
si bien su freno espumas, ilustraba
las columnas Etón que erigió el griego,
do el carro de la luz sus ruedas lava. (43.337–40)

(With smoking breath, and uttering snorts of fire,
Aethon, his bit full of foam, illuminated the
columns erected by the Greek (Hercules),
where light's chariot washes its wheels.)

The sun's horses, all smoke and fire, announce the entrance of the fierce giant, who from a high, wild rock overlooking the seashore – "a blind lighthouse" and "a mute watchtower" (43.344), representing the Cyclops's erotic blindness – plays his pipes with the "bellows of his mighty breath" (44.348).

Unbeknownst to him, Galatea listens to his music in fear and trembling, wishing to merge with her landscape, this time in a physical diminishment in search of safety: to be "a tiny flower, a humble weed, a bit of earth" (breve flor, hierba humilde, tierra poca), rather than what she is now, a "vine" (vid lasciva) bonded to her "new tree" (nuevo tronco) in her secluded space with Acis (44.349–52). The text comments how the caverns and hills, forewarned by the "zampoña ruda" (the crude pipes), are drawn into Polyphemus's ominous, discordant soundscape, "assaulted" by the thunder of the giant's voice as he begins his song. Full of sadness and praise, it entreats Galatea for her presence. Celebrating her beauty, he calls on her to leave the sea and join him at the shore. A gilding performance, a bit of theatre, and acts of idolatry bring together familiar images of her foot stepping on the sand:

Pisa la arena, que en la arena adoro
cuantas el blanco pie conchas platea,
cuyo bello contacto puede hacerlas,
sin concebir rocío, parir perlas. (47.373–6)

(Step on the sand, for on the sand I adore
all the shells silvered by your white foot,

whose lovely touch can make them,
without conceiving dew, give birth to pearls.)

Those words, identifying Polyphemus with the failed suitors who worshiped Galatea at the seashore, where they placed their gifts, foreshadow the failure of his song.

As a melancholic, he is himself a figure of liminality, possessing the in-betweenness that Marsilio Ficino ascribes to melancholia: a deep sense of loss, both physical and psychological, "an affliction of the soul" accompanied by both sorrow and exultation. Ascribed above all to the contemplative brooder, it is a sign of genius, of inspiration and creativity. According to Ficino's astral magic, Saturn, the highest of the planets under whose influence the melancholic is born, is a dark and malevolent planet but also the "*iuvans pater* of men of intellect" (Klibansky, Panofsky and Saxl 1964, 254).[16] Ficino gave shape to melancholia as the exclusive subjectivity of the man of letters according to a double formula, as does modern psychoanalysis. In *Mourning and Melancholia*, Sigmund Freud writes of that double-sided nature of the melancholic. He is "poor and empty," one who reveals "an extraordinary diminution in his self-regard" (1978, 14:246), but also a narcissist, exuberant in his eloquence; insistent in his self-criticism, he needs to speak out, to find "satisfaction in self-exposure," a kind of "narcissistic pleasure" in self-display. "It is what we call an *accredited pathology*," writes Juliana Schiesari, "justified by the heightened sense of conscience that the melancholic is said to display ostentatiously" (1992, 9; emphasis in the original). Placing himself at the centre of a scene of loss, and eloquently voicing his discontent, Freud's melancholic, much like Ficino's, projects himself as someone of exceptional qualities.

Góngora's Polyphemus belongs to this Ficinian-Freudian double scene. Perched on his promontory, the solitary Cyclops takes pleasure in displaying his sorrow and sense of loss in an exhibitionistic performance that reveals a praiseworthy lover and poet. Galatea, a typical *donna petrosa* of Dantean and Petrarchan origin, causes his inner diminishment, evident in the sighs and tears in his declaration of pain: "Sorda hija del mar, cuyas orejas / a mis gemidos son *rocas* al viento" (48.377–8, my emphasis; Deaf daughter of the sea, whose ears are to my moans *rocks* against the wind). Yet, alongside this broken self, the slightly ridiculous and not so delicate seducer fashions an inflated, narcissistic image of himself in a singular spectacle for Galatea; flaunting his lineage as the son of Neptune, he proclaims his name "Polifemo te llama, no te escondas" (51.405). Admiring his voice (48.383–4), he portrays himself as a poet, his pen a finger writing his sorrow in the sky: "y en los cielos, desde esta roca, puedo / escribir mis desdichas con el dedo" (52.415–16). A Cyclopean man of letters, he would write in the heavens as on a blank page what he now laments with his voice.[17]

The rock from which he speaks becomes a site of recollection, a space of the imagination, where he portrays himself as a figure of gentility and courtesy. He tells Galatea how he transformed his cave into a social space of safety and hospitality, where he hosted a shipwrecked Genoese and engaged in gift-giving, offering the "peregrino" some of his "choicest fruits" in return for luxurious crafted objects from the Orient that have washed ashore from the lost ship: a carved "ivory bow" and a "delicate quiver, / both from a famous craftsman, gifted / by a Malaccan king to a goddess of Java" (57–58.453–60). The gifts are for Galatea, though his best gift, his solar eye, is most personal, a fetish to be admired and perhaps loved. His "gifting" is executed through self-praise in a memorable act of self-display in front of a mirror, the reflecting surface that is part of a gilded landscape: "espejo de zafiro fue luciente / la playa azul, de la persona mía" (53.419–20; the blue sea was a shining sapphire mirror where my figure was reflected):

"Miréme, y lucir vi un sol en mi frente,
cuando en el cielo un ojo se veía:
neutra el agua dudaba a cuál fe preste,
o al cielo humano, o al cíclope celeste." (53.421–4)

("I looked at myself, and I saw a sun shining on my brow,
just as in the sky there was but one eye:
the water, undecided, was doubtful which to believe,
the human heaven or the celestial Cyclops.")

If, for Galatea and Acis, landscape is a medium of exchange and a site of "visual appropriation" for the construction of identity, it is the same for the Cyclops but with a difference. Living in isolation and whirling narcissistically in his monocular orbit, Polyphemus has a visual exchange with his own image. Like Narcissus at his pool, he is at once subject and object, spectator and spectacle, his reflection being not of his appearance but of an imagined, ideal persona. His use of the mirror follows conventional lines of inquiry, as an instrument for self-imaging and, by extension, for introspection and the construction of an interiorized model of selfhood. For Leonardo da Vinci, the mirror was "the master of painters," "the secret accomplice" that no self-portraitist could do without (Woods-Marsden 1998, 31). For Leon Battista Alberti, it was the site where reality and illusion, truth and appearance, were most intricately intertwined. In Polyphemus's dynamic discursive space, self-love and self-knowledge converge with self-deception.

For the rejected Polyphemus, this specular moment is an instance of healing, when he can imagine himself in full mastery, complete and restored, and where he proclaims himself a "celestial Cyclops." Having robbed the sky of its sun, he places it on his forehead, reducing the sun to a mere eye. In the process, as Kathleen Dolan suggests, "he creates a myth of the self, a fantasy of a solar, divine identity which is a source of light and vision" (1990, 91). "Miréme" is a call to Galatea to see him as he wants to be seen: not as a monstrous one-eyed Cyclops but as a heavenly being whose eye, seductive and irresistible in its luminosity, is a thing of beauty. In effect he seeks to rectify Galatea's image of him. He seeks as well to refocus the lyric speaker's portrayal of his eye as *almost* but not quite like the sun: "un ojo ilustra el orbe de su frente, / émulo *casi* del mayor lucero" (7.51–2, my emphasis; a single eye adorns the orb of his forehead, which shines *almost* like the sun, the brightest star). He makes the sea an accomplice in his self-celebration, with the waters, in indecision, validating his vision of himself as a celestial Cyclops: "neutra el agua dudaba a cuál fe preste, / o al cielo humano, o al cíclope celeste." Yet his ideal image is an illusion, his wholeness and harmony a fantasy. No matter how luminous, his eye as fetish is a mark of his monstrosity, and so a mark of his vulnerability and one of the reasons for Galatea's rejection. The fragmenting force of desire has indelibly marked him, and so his psychic instability is manifest in the very medium that serves for his celebration. Although a site of epistemological discovery, the mirror as mediator calls into question the act of self-knowledge, challenging and complicating the very act of self-definition. Its reflective surface yields but a simulacrum of the self, a doubling that undermines knowledge of the self and, consequently, a true sense of personal identity. The space of luminous self-display is a space for deception.

Ultimately Polyphemus's ideal image is built on words, a splendidly modulated discourse in which he creates an identity at odds with his actions. In making his imagined exterior beauty conform to an inner beauty, he claims that love transforms him. But when goats eating his vines interrupt his lament, his gentleness disappears, and his violence is unleashed in a shower of fierce shouts and stones (59.470–1). A seductive performance is betrayed by a monstrous nature.[18] No longer in the realm of his narcissistic self-reflexivity, the Cyclops turns his sight outward to the lovers, who are running towards the sea, their bond broken by fear:

Viendo el fiero jayán, con paso mudo
correr al mar la fugitiva nieve
(que a tanta vista el líbico desnudo
registra el campo de su adarga breve)
y al garzón viendo, cuantas mover pudo
celoso trueno, antiguas hayas mueve:
tal, antes que la opaca nube rompa,
previene rayo fulminante trompa. (61.481–8)

(When the giant witnesses the fleeting snow
slipping silently towards the sea
(for his sight is so acute he can discover
the patterns on the naked Libyans' shield)
and sees the youth as well, he emits a bellow
so resonant it shakes the mightiest tree:
just so, when the dense cloud's about to burst,
a clap of thunder heralds the fatal blast.)

The visual field offers Polyphemus the spectacle of a collapse that will translate into death. The giant's vision, which had been fixed on himself for a narcissistic celebration, is now directed at the lovers. His vision is acute – he can see across the Mediterranean to Libya, discerning patterns on the shields of naked natives – and predatory, as the darkness within him erupts in jealous fury.[19] Tearing part of his rock, he hurls it at his rival, crushing him:

Con vïolencia desgajó infinita,
la mayor punta de la excelsa roca,
que al joven, sobre quien la precipita,
urna es mucha, pirámide no poca. (62.489–92)

(With irresistible force he tore away
the thickest point of his mighty rock,
which at once became for the one on whom it lay
an outsize urn, a pyramid of no mean proportions.)

The scene of death, in its material turn, becomes a sepulchral space for Acis, who, entombed as if memorialized for an instant, ironically merges with the giant's landscape. The rock is both a funerary urn, where ashes of the dead were placed in ancient times, and a pyramid, which recalls the tombs of the Egyptians. As for the Cyclops, night has overcome him. This is after all his true realm. His cave, depicted at the outset as a melancholy void (6.42), remains his dark and ominous emblem. This formidable one-eyed monster, belligerent son of Neptune, is configured through interplay between the celestial and the terrestrial: he reaches up to the sky and down to fierce subterranean depths. In the end the despondency of rejection blends with the rage of jealousy. The darkness of Polyphemus, with his desire not only rejected but betrayed, bursts out, as potent as his vision: the melancholic and the monster fuse to kill and destroy. Transgressing boundaries, his malefic vision is directed inwards, and a magnificent song of the self fails to persuade. Galatea, in tears, and Acis pray to the ocean deities, who save Acis by transforming his bleeding body into a river through an act of gilding: his blood becomes "pure crystal," and his white bones, now flowing silver, lick the flowers and reach the shore, silvering the sand (63.496–504).

The *Polifemo*'s enchaining landscapes rewrite the ancient myth as a material lyric in which each frame captures a unique lived space that is produced by a defining performative act: the count's hunting at dawn in his forest, Acis and Galatea's midday erotic encounter in the *locus amoenus*, and Polyphemus's narcissistic self-reflections and violent acts at dusk. If the count's space is animated by hunting and storytelling, and the lovers' by gift-giving and visual exchange, the space of Polyphemus, devoid of human interaction, engages only himself. The equilibrium of spaces existing side by side is shattered by the monster's breeching of the pastoral idyll.

Coda: A Cornucopian Space

The *Polifemo*, conspicuously centred on the abundance of material objects, functions at multiple levels: lexical, semantic, rhetorical, and spatial. Sicily, where the action takes place, is a land of abundance, a horn of plenty – first signalled by the cup of Bacchus, the cart of Ceres, and the garden of Pomona (18.13–44). The social order of pastoral Sicily, centred on the making and gathering of products of the land, yields its distinctive pastoral space. Like the count's space, created in his village and forest, the island's bucolic space is a relational, practised place, but of a non-aristocratic origin produced by vintners, farmers, and fruit growers, who make or gather humble products. There is something here of what John Beverley detected in the *Soledades*, a work that displays an "interest in the ways ordinary people make their living," which is illustrated by "the simple curve of a wooden cup turned on a lathe," by "the freshness and thickness of curded milk," or by "the *invención rara* of a spoon" (1980, 1–2). Beverley writes, "It seems more a language whose own concern with technique is bound up in the qualities of the simple objects of labor or consumption it is describing, objects which, like Góngora's images, are devices for *capturing* and *containing*" (2; emphasis in the original).

In the *Polifemo*, containers stand for abundance, a sense of plenitude, foregrounded by the copious wicker basket of the fruit grower: "de la Copia [...] el cuerno vierte el hortelano, entero, / sobre la mimbre que tejió prolija, si artificiosa no, su honesta hija" (20.155–60; the horn of plenty ... the fruit grower pours entire upon the wicker woven, slowly, if not artfully, by his chaste daughter). The metatextual *copia* defines the poem's distinctive baroque fullness, particularly its semantic connotation. In *The Cornucopian Text*, Terence Cave writes, "the semantic field of *copia* includes not only the notion of abundance itself but also the place where abundance is to be found, or, more strictly, the place and its contents: one of the particular senses of *copia* is 'treasure chest,' 'hoard,' or 'store'" (1979, 6). Pointing to both a place and its contents – objects denoting abundance and an abundance of objects – the treasure chest becomes a distinctive cultural space, where individual and social identities are constructed. The wicker basket as a "treasure chest" of fruit, a Sicily as horn of plenty in little, becomes in its rusticity and lack of artifice the space in which the humble owner's identity is constituted and represented. This spatial dynamic combining a material man-made object with personal identity echoes in the bag of the goatherd Polyphemus, which, bursting at the seams with fruit, mimics his brute force, and in Acis's refined containers for his gifts to Galatea: the white wicker for the almonds, the green reeds for the butter, and the small but skilfully shaped cork for the honeycomb, which represent the delicacy of the sophisticated seducer.

The spaces created, large and small, have in common a rhetorical exuberance, another type of *copia* at the level of writerly performance, which Cave defines as an "articulate energy" of "speech in action." A synonym for eloquence, *copia* stands for "a rich multi-faceted discourse springing from a fertile mind and powerfully affecting its recipient. At this level, its value lies precisely in the broadness of its figurative register" (1979, 5).[20]

Ancient rhetoric, particularly that of Cicero and Quintilian, uses this sense of *copia* in the context of the fundamental play of things (*res*) and words (*verba*). If *res* is subsumed under *inventio* – the creation of an effective and compelling argument – *verba* is subsumed under *elocutio*, the domain of style, tropes, and other figures of speech (Cave 1979, 5–6). The *Polifemo*'s inventive, copious discourse has as its basis a clever combination of things and words, a way of establishing the poet's distinctive baroque voice in an ingenious writerly performance that is exclusively his own. Sicilian abundance in objects and their gilding reveal the "articulate energy" and fertile speech singled out by Cave. The variety of containers reflect a layering of copious discourse as a layering of the island's humble products like variations on a theme in three keys through that most artificial of tropes, catachresis, in which these products become gleaming, luxurious things. First there is a long shot of the landscape, where goddesses are engaged in an unveiling of plenitude, the riches of the land: "si en la [vega de Ceres] granos de oro llueve, / copos nieva en [la cumbre de Pales] mil de lana" (19.147–8; if on [Ceres's plain] grains of gold rain, a thousand snowflakes of wool fall on Pales's heights). Then there is a close shot to the workers who toil on the land to yield their products: "cuantos siegan oro, esquilan nieve, / o en pipas guardan la exprimida grana" (19.149–50; all those who reap gold, shear snow, or store the purple wine), the products that become the splendid gifts offered by the suitors at Galatea's seashore altar. And in the third shot, the gilding of these objects of the land finds an echo in the precious artefact that is the body of Galatea, constructed by layers of cultural objects of splendour, jewels, gems, and precious stones, as the poet extends his baroque gilding from the count's rural estate to the humble products of the land to the human body itself, which conform to Paul Julian Smith on the *Polifemo*: "there can be no nakedness unclothed by culture, no instinct uncompromised by textuality" (1989, 61).

The weaving of the fruit grower's wicker basket by his daughter takes us to the artifice of the text itself, to its making in yet another type of *copia*. Roland Barthes's memorable phrase, "*textus*, from which text derives, means 'woven'" (1979, 76), defines *Polifemo* as a cornucopian text woven of fragments and allusions from ancient letters, from Homer, Theocritus, Virgil, and Ovid – "encyclopedic treasure-houses (*copiae*) of knowledge and of rhetorical ... ornament"

(Cave 1979, 174) – as well as from Italian and Spanish sources. Amidst all the abundance, however, there is a sense of "rupture," an "emptiness" between the unfolding of fullness and plenitude and its textual telling that denotes a collapse, a "falling away" from plenitude: the suitors' failed courtship, the unanswered call of Polyphemus's song, and the "death" of Acis, his love adventure swiftly cut short by a monstrous boulder hurled by the jealous Cyclops.[21] Yet for Acis, the "fall" is qualified. His transformation into a river marks a new beginning with Galatea in her domain, where her mother, the Oceanid-nymph Doris, welcomes him as her son-in-law.

Chapter Four

Staging Myth

The mythological paintings that Juan de Arguijo (c. 1565–1623) commissioned in 1601 for the library ceiling of his palace in Seville survive as the earliest example in Spain of a genre of painting popularized in sixteenth-century Italy. They were part of an original project to stage the mythological scenes with poems that served as commentaries for an audience of humanists who met in the library. In two sonnets he gives voice to the panels of young men going beyond the bounds: Phaëthon, who falls to his death from his father's chariot; and Ganymede, who is carried up to Olympus by Jupiter, transformed into an eagle. The uniqueness of Arguijo's project lies in a triadic performance. By casting ancient myths in ceiling paintings, which are interpreted by poems that speak for them, and by staging the two interrelated media for dialogic exchange with his academy of artists and scholars, Arguijo created an original form of the material lyric, one that combined written text, a pictorial scene, and a learned audience for a dynamic cultural performance.

W.J.T. Mitchell offers a fruitful way for discussing the interplay between image, word, and object in Arguijo's library. "What is an object?" he asks. "What is its relation to a subject and to the words and images that subjects construct to make objects intelligible?" (1994, 241). Intelligibility, in Mitchell's sense, is at the core of my analysis here, for Arguijo's sonnets are not strictly ekphrastic, that is, linguistic representations of pictorial scenes. They act primarily as commentaries that make the paintings intelligible to viewers as if they were displayed in a museum. To Mitchell's insight I add Jerome McGann's observation that "texts are produced and reproduced under specific social and institutional conditions, and hence ... every text, including those that may appear to be purely private, is a social text. This view entails a corollary understanding, that a 'text' is not [just] a 'material thing' but a material event … a point in time (or a moment in space) where certain *communicative interchanges* are being practiced" (1991, 21; my emphasis).[1] In this sense I take the interplay among the texts (the sonnets), the material (the ceiling paintings), and the social context (the academy) as a transactional act in which members of the academy, by viewing the paintings through the prism of Arguijo's poems, transform the poet's library into a stage for the performance of a cultural memory.

Arguijo's ceiling panels are notable for their depiction of mythological subjects when mythological paintings on canvas were rare in Spanish baroque art because Church censorship discouraged both ecclesiastical and lay patrons from commissioning works involving nudity (Brown 1978, 72). Yet kings and nobles commissioned mythological paintings from foreign artists, Italian and Flemish in particular, and displayed them prominently in their homes and at court. Philip II famously commissioned paintings from Tintoretto and Veronese and had a special affection (as did his father, Charles V) for Titian, who sent him a *Danaë* in 1554 while he was still crown prince, a *Rape of Europa* in 1562, and a lascivious *Venus* in 1567, which hung in El Pardo, his hunting lodge, from which it takes its name, the Pardo Venus. Years later, when Philip III heard of the fire at El Pardo, he was relieved to learn that since the Titian *Venus* "had not burned, the others mattered little" (que como aquella pintura no se hubiese quemado, que las demás importaba poco; Gallego 1984, 51). The high nobility followed the royal example. The Duke of Villahermosa, for one, commissioned copies of Italian paintings on mythological subjects from the Flemish artist Esquert (Angulo Íñiguez 1952, 15). Yet not all mythological paintings were imported or copied. There was in fact an important production of mythological scenes in Spain by Spanish and foreign artists, but those were largely relegated to the margins, to murals and frescoes in public buildings and private residences; few have survived, and still fewer have been inventoried (López Torrijos 1985, 16).

Arguijo engaged the ancient myths while living a highly public life in Seville, a bustling city of wealth and sophistication (Vranich 1985, 13–28). His father and father-in-law had acquired fortunes through trade with the Indies and, like the local nobles, collected paintings and artefacts for their elegant residences. Fernando Enríquez de Ribera, the third duke of Alcalá, was an avid collector and bibliophile, and his palace, the Casa de Pilatos, was filled with Roman antiquities, including magnificent copies of a lost work by Phidias, the *Minerva Lemnia* (Brown 1978, 38–9). Like the duke, Arguijo engaged in a wide-ranging cultural *translatio* with Italy, importing paintings and antique statuary. Their homes would have been private museums were it not for the academies, loose organizations of writers, scholars, and artists who met to discuss literary and artistic interests. The most prestigious academy in Seville was hosted by Francisco Pacheco (1564–1644), cathedral canon and distinguished local painter, who continued the academy of Juan de Mal Lara, one of the earliest in Spain, which was founded in the mid-sixteenth century.[2] The Duke of Alcalá attended Pacheco's academy but also welcomed his humanist friends to his own academy, held in his library. Arguijo may have participated in Pacheco's academy but, according to a contemporary biographer, decided to form his own "and gather poets, musicians, and men of wit in his house. Thus he was known by all those in the realm who practiced arts" (*Memorias sevillanas;* cited in Brown 1978, 40). The academies made Seville a destination for leading writers and artists in search of patrons and fellowship beyond the royal court.

The Ceiling Paintings

Painted ceilings were popular in Italy, especially in Venice, which was known for the number of religious and private buildings with ceilings painted by the likes of Tintoretto and Giulio Romano. Very few private residences with mythological scenes survive today, however, beyond the ones painted by Tintoretto (Schulz 1968, 117–23). Perhaps the most famous and influential extant examples of painted ceilings in Italy were in Vasari's house in Arezzo (1548), which he describes in his *Vite* and which may have inspired Arguijo's ceiling, despite its entirely different iconographical program (Lleó Cañal 1999, 176–7).[3]

As was customary, Arguijo, the commissioning patron, would have chosen the program for the scenes in his ceiling panels, which were painted by Alonso Vázquez (Serrera 1996, 41). Jonathan Brown has suggested that Francisco de Medina, who corrected Arguijo's poetry manuscripts and possessed the classical erudition that informed the paintings, might have been the author of the ceiling's pictorial program (1978, 78). The paintings are arranged in a rectangle consisting of five discrete scenes, a large central panel and four smaller ones in each corner. The central panel depicts an Assembly of the Gods, with Jupiter occupying a privileged place at one end of the panel and surrounded by his attributes: a sceptre in his left hand, a bolt of lightning under his left foot, and an eagle alongside (fig. 4.1). As the father of the gods, and the figure of ultimate authority, he plays a major role in the fates of Phäethon and Ganymede, who appear on the two smaller panels opposite him, separated by the inscription: "Genio et musis dicatum" (Dedicated to genius and the muses), with the year 1601. In smaller panels at bottom left, Astraea, the goddess of justice, holds a sword and a balance, and at bottom right is a personification of Envy.[4] In one of Vasari's ceiling paintings, in a central octagon in the Sala del Trionfo della Virtù, a personified Envy, an old hag surrounded by serpents, lies under the feet of Excellence, who seizes Fortune by the hair in a typical psychomacy (the battle of virtues and vices) (Vasari 1996, 1:1046).[5] In Arguijo's painting, Envy also is pictured as an old hag, but she is alone in her panel and, as if in internal struggle, tears snakes from her hair.

Arguijo's painted ceiling inspired the Duke of Alcalá (1603) and the archbishop of Seville (1604) to commission paintings for the ceilings of their palaces, the Casa de Pilatos and the Palacio Arzobispal, which also survive. Their arrangements, however, differ fundamentally from Arguijo's.[6] The duke commissioned Pacheco, the most prominent painter in Seville at the time, to paint the ceiling. Several figures, among them a Phaëthon and a semi-nude Ganymede, are similar to those in Arguijo's paintings, which serve as models. Michelangelo's nude Ganymede also may have served as a model because Pacheco owned a copy that had belonged to Arias Montano (Lleó Cañal 1979, 57). Pacheco gave a prominent role to Hercules in the assembly of the gods (a role missing in Arguijo's painting), which represented virtue and hard work, as a mirror for the young duke. The paintings for the archbishop are of an entirely different order: fifty-two Old and New Testament scenes for his *salón principal*, and twenty-seven decorative scenes for the *prelado* gallery (Fernández López 1999, 159–71; Valdivieso and Serrera, 1979). For the archbishop and the duke, the paintings were essentially decorative. They lack both the poetic commentaries that animate Arguijo's paintings and the critical combination of poems, paintings, and academy that made his library the site of a stimulating cultural experience.

Phaëthon

Phaëthon tumbling out of the skies with chariot and horses (fig. 4.2) was a familiar subject in paintings, emblems, and illustrations of the time, making it impossible to determine the pictorial source of the rendition on Arguijo's ceiling. The foundational text is Ovid's *Metamorphoses* (1984, 1:2.131–328), in which Phaëthon, son of the sun god Helios and the Oceanid Clymene, seeks confirmation of his divine birth. To prove to the world that he is Helios's son, he asks his father permission to drive the golden chariot. Having promised his son anything he desired, a reluctant Helios grants his wish but counsels him to steer a middle course; too high, he will burn up the skies, or too low, he will destroy the earth: "in the middle is the safest path" (2:136–7). Phaëthon,

Figure 4.1 *Assembly of the Gods*, ceiling painting, Casa de Arguijo, 1601. Museo de Bellas Artes, Seville. Fondo Gráfico Archivo IAPH. Autor: José Manuel Santos Madrid.

Figure 4.2 *Fall of Phaëthon* (detail), ceiling painting, Casa de Arguijo, 1601. Museo de Bellas Artes, Seville. Fondo Gráfico Archivo IAPH. Autor: José Manuel Santos Madrid.

however, lacks the strength to manage the horses' reins, and as the solar chariot traverses the heavens, it careens out of control, threatening to set the earth on fire. To prevent that catastrophe, Jupiter strikes the chariot with a thunderbolt, and Phaëthon falls to his death, punished for his foolish undertaking.

Jacques Lacan's psychoanalytic theory offers useful ways to interpret Phaëton's relation to his father, Helios, and to Jupiter, the supreme deity among the gods. Helios and Jupiter, agents of law and order, stand for what Lacan calls the "nom (non)-du-père," the name of the father, the forbidding "no" of paternal authority and as such the power of language and culture to establish boundaries, including boundaries for desire (1977, 65–8). Phaëthon perishes, lost in the whirling fictions of his Imaginary, the realm of the narcissistic ego-ideal and "the scene of a desperate delusional attempt to be and to remain 'what one is'" (Bowie 1991, 92). His presumption is punished by Jupiter, the divine father and ruler of heaven and earth. In Ovid's narrative, Naiads bury his still burning body and carve an epitaph on his tomb, which praises his daring: "Here Phaëthon lies: in his father's chariot he fared, / and though he greatly failed, more greatly dared" (Ovid 1984, 1:2.327–8). Helios, sick with grief, hides his face, while a distraught Clymene wanders the earth, seeking her son's body. Finding the Naiads' tomb inscribed with his name, she drenches it with tears; her daughters, the Heliades, join her in weeping and are later turned into poplars (1:2.329–66).

Arguijo amplifies the Naiads' celebration in his sonnet, which becomes the inscription to his painting:

Pudo quitarte el nuevo atrevimiento,
bello hijo del Sol, la dulce vida;
la memoria no pudo, qu'extendida
dejó la fama de tan alto intento.
Glorioso aunque infelice pensamiento
desculpó la carrera mal regida;
y del paterno carro la caída
subió tu nombre a más ilustre asiento.
En tal demanda al mundo aseguraste
que de Apolo eras hijo, pues pudiste
alcanzar dél la empresa a que aspiraste.
Término ponga a su lamento triste
Climene, si la gloria que ganaste
excede al bien que por osar perdiste. (Arguijo 1971, 55)

(A novel daring could take away
your sweet life, beautiful son of the Sun,
but it could not take away the memory
that brought fame to so noble an undertaking.
A glorious though unhappy thought
excused a badly guided course,
and the fall from your father's chariot
raised your name to a more illustrious seat.
With such a venture you assured the world
that you were Apollo's son, because you
obtained from him the goal you aspired to.
May Clymene end her sad lament,
since the glory you won exceeds
the good you lost by your daring.)

The sonnet's praise follows a popular early modern interpretation that reads Phaëthon's courageous daring as worthy of glory and fame.[7] From the reluctant father he obtained what he desired, and through his fall his name rises ("subió tu nombre") to a loftier place, imprinting his fame on the world's collective memory. Arguijo's sonnet legitimizes the fall brought about by Jupiter as a rite of passage into the symbolic order, the world of language and culture. In a significant detail the sonnet does not mention the Greek sun god Helios. Phaëton's father is here Phoebus Apollo, the Graeco-Roman sun god, who appears among the Olympians in the ceiling painting and who is the god of poetry and literary renown. The ceiling inscription, "Dedicated to genius and the muses" – the goddesses who inspire the arts, literature, and science – alerts the viewer to the scene's symbolic significance.

Ovid's Naiads had made Phaëthon worthy of being "written," rescuing him from oblivion by inscribing an epitaph on his tomb. The sonnet's ending echoes the Naiads' epitaph in the poet's message to Clymene, telling her to cease her mourning and lament, and in a sense encouraging her to accept the epitaph's celebration of her son's undertaking.

In the tradition of ancient tomb inscriptions Phaëthon's epitaph is a site of pilgrimage and discourse, assuring him a place in memory and history. Like the Naiads, Arguijo deems Phaëthon worthy of being "written" but goes one step further: Phaëthon is also worthy of being "painted," memorialized in another public space, the poet's library, the space of the academy, the humanist world that privileges pagan arts and letters. Inscribed on material surfaces – paper and wood – Phaëthon's memory is saved, in Roger Chartier's familiar words, from time and oblivion (2007, vii). If the panel showcases the consequences of Phaëthon's answer to the father, his fame visually there in paint, Arguijo the poet finds in the ceiling a way to showcase his own fame. His coat of arms, appearing between the panels of Astraea and Envy, there in paint, stages his name and lineage. If Quevedo's retreat in la Torre de Juan Abat is a private space where he listens to the ancients with "his eyes," Arguijo's library resides in a public arena for display and performance for the eyes of his humanist companions, leaving Arguijo's own imprint on collective memory. Arguijo's ceiling painting, with his coat of arms among the gods and the muses in plain view of humanist friends, emulated Vasari's Chamber of Fame, the room at the entrance to his house in Arezzo, where Fame is painted on the ceiling, surrounded by portraits of the leading artists of Vasari's time (De Girolamo Cheney 2006, 91–100).

Ganymede

The ceiling's companion painting, the *Rape of Ganymede* (fig. 4.3) also deals with transgression, this time that of the god. In Ovid's *Metamorphoses* the myth appears as a brief narrative told by Orpheus, who sings "of boys beloved by gods" (1984, 2:10.152–3). Jupiter, who falls in love with Ganymede, assumes the form of an eagle, a bird with the power to "bear his thunderbolts" (10:158), in order to abduct his prey. In Orpheus's words, "without delay he cleft the air on his lying wings and stole away the Trojan boy, who even now, though against the will of Juno, mingles the nectar and attends the cups of Jove" (10:159–61). The best-known and most copied representation of the myth in early modern Europe was Michelangelo's drawing of *Ganymede* (1533), one of four drawings of mythological scenes sent by the artist to his young friend, the handsome Roman nobleman Tommaso de' Cavalieri (fig. 4.4).[8]

Michelangelo places the eagle and the boy in a position of reciprocity, as their twisting, interlocked bodies ascend in parallel, with the eagle's talons gripping Ganymede's spreading legs, a sign of the eagle's intent and the boy's erotic submission.[9] Vasari, perhaps to deflect attention from the blatant eroticism, offers a pedagogical purpose for the drawing: "[Michelangelo] made, to the end that [Tommaso] might learn to draw," he writes, "many … superb drawings of divinely beautiful heads, designed in black and red chalk; and then he drew for him a Ganymede rapt to Heaven by Jove's Eagle, a Tityus with the Vulture devouring his heart, the Chariot of the Sun falling with Phaëthon into the Po, and a Bacchanal of children, which are all in themselves most

Figure 4.3 *Rape of Ganymede* (detail), ceiling painting, Casa de Arguijo, 1601. Museo de Bellas Artes, Seville. Fondo Gráfico Archivo IAPH. Autor: José Manuel Santos Madrid.

Figure 4.4 *Ganymede*, copy after Michelangelo, sixteenth century, black chalk on off-white antique laid paper. Harvard Art Museums/Fogg Museum © President and Fellows of Harvard College.

rare things, and drawings the likes of which have never been seen" (1996, 2:737). Tommaso shared Vasari's enthusiasm for the drawings, writing in a letter to Michelangelo: "Mi pigliarò almanco doi hore del giorno piacere in contemplare doi vostri desegni [...] quanto più li miro, tanto più mi piacciono" (Poggi, Barocchi, and Ristori 1965–83, 3:445; I will take at least two hours a day to enjoy contemplating your two drawings (the *Tityus* and the *Ganymede*) ... the more I study them, the more they please me).

The intent of Michelangelo's drawings, which was left unsaid in his correspondence with Tommaso, is found in his sonnets, which reference sexuality as well as the ecstasy of Neoplatonic love, a popular interpretation imposed on the *Ganymede* drawing in the manner of Landino's explanation of Dante's *Purgatorio* 9. Just as Arguijo's poem is an inscription for the Phaëthon painting, Michelangelo's letters and sonnets serve as inscriptions to his drawings, deciphering their meaning for Tommaso. Leonard Barkan points to the drawing and the sonnets as a project of the artist's "love for Cavalieri but also of the purity of his passion" (1991, 83).[10] Michelangelo's drawing of Ganymede "is designed to order, or perhaps tame" the "troubling" aspects of the artist's desire; "put another way, it is designed to infold them in a symbol or a myth" (83). But, adds Barkan, no amount of "image making" can suppress the erotic import. Thus, while Ganymede's serenity in face and body connects the drawing to the tradition of the dream vision, of divine contemplation, as in Dante's depiction of Ganymede in *Purgatorio*, serenity also points to sexual passivity, the conventional role of the catamite (linked etymologically to the Latin form of the name Ganymede), in which the boy and the eagle are linked in sexual intimacy (84–5).

Arguijo's Ganymede belongs to a different project. While the boy appears in a full frontal pose, the figure's iconographical details differ sharply from those in Michelangelo's drawing. In a concession to ecclesiastical authority, a cloth covers the boy's genital area, and, unlike Michelangelo's Ganymede, whose face is tranquil and acquiescent, Arguijo's Ganymede seems to be struggling in the eagle's embrace. As the bird's claws hold tightly his right leg, the boy's twisted torso and outstretched arm turn away from the eagle's beak, and his mouth grimaces in a gesture of distaste. Arguijo's portrait is of a reluctant, frightened Ganymede. His sonnet captures the moment of the boy's fear and the erotic tension, which is offered from the eagle's point of view. In Ovid's text the eagle is silent. Here it speaks, wooing Ganymede in flight:

No temas, o bellísimo troyano,
viendo que arrebatado en nuevo vuelo
con corvas uñas te levanta al cielo
la feroz ave por el aire vano.
¿Nunca has oído el nombre soberano
del alto Olimpo, la piedad y el celo
de Júpiter, que da la pluvia al suelo
y arma con rayos la tonante mano;
A cuyas sacras aras humillado
gruesos toros ofrece el Teucro en Ida,
implorando remedio a sus querellas?
El mismo soy. No al'águila eres dado
en despojo; mi amor te trae. Olvida
tu amada Troya y sube a las estrellas. (Arguijo 1971, 69)

(Do not fear, oh most beautiful Trojan,
seeing that a fierce bird with hooked claws
carries you off in novel flight, lifting you
to the heavens through the empty air.
Have you not heard the sovereign name
of high Olympus, the compassion and zeal
of Jupiter, who sends rain to earth and arms
with thunderbolts his powerful hand;
At whose sacred altars the kneeling
Teucer [Trojan] offers hefty bulls in Ida,
imploring remedies for his complaints?
I am he. You are not given to the eagle
as bits of flesh; my love brings you.
Forget your beloved Troy and rise to the stars.)

Arguijo's sonnet is entitled "Del rapto de Ganimedes, traducción de Fracastorio [*sic*]," to acknowledge his rendering of a fragment of *De anima* by Girolamo Fracastoro (1478–1553). The sonnet is not a simple translation, however.[11] Fracastoro's text offers a popular Neoplatonic interpretation of the abduction of Ganymede, much like Michelangelo's, with an ascent of the soul to the astral sphere and the joys of heaven. Fracastoro relied on Cristoforo Landino's 1481 commentary on Dante's *Purgatorio* 9, which explains that Ganymede appears in a dream as the Mind, the highest faculty of the human soul, and his abduction represents the rise of the Mind to ecstatic contemplation of the divine: "Ganymede, then, would signify the *mens humana*, beloved by Jupiter, that is: the Supreme Being ... Jupiter, realizing that the Mind is in the forest – that is, remote from mortal things, transports it to heaven by means of the eagle ...; and being removed, or as Plato says, divorced from the body, and forgetting corporeal things, it concentrates entirely on contemplating the secrets of Heaven" (cited in Panofsky 1967, 215).[12]

Arguijo takes a different stance. Translating eleven lines of Fracastoro's text, he lifts the fragment out of its Neoplatonic context and the connection to the dream vision, to offer instead Jupiter's speech as a purely erotic persuasion, a coaxing of a beautiful yet reluctant male beloved, in graceful hendecasyllables that contrast with Fracastoro's belaboured hexameters. It is a carefully crafted seduction: in a *captatio benevolentiae*, Jupiter tries to allay Ganymede's fear: "no temas" are his first words, as he describes the eagle from the boy's point of view, "viendo que arrebatado en nuevo vuelo / con corvas uñas te levanta al cielo / la feroz ave." Jupiter flatters Ganymede with "bellísimo," which adds a sensual, homoerotic dimension not in Fracastoro. He proceeds to reveal himself, boasting his compassion and zeal ("la piedad y el celo"), two traits not found in Fracastoro, and his power in ritual and cult. The exhortation ends climatically with the narcissistic "El mismo soy," followed by the justification of the abduction: "No al'águila eres dado / en despojo; mi amor te trae." By rendering Fracastoro's *praeda* as *despojo*, Arguijo stresses the eagle's predatory nature, which is not unleashed on Ganymede, for whom Jupiter reserves only his love. He finally coaxes, "Olvida / tu amada Troya y sube a las estrellas." Unlike Phaëthon, who disobeyed his father, Ganymede must say "yes" to his father in order to ascend in glory "to the stars." Here it is Jupiter who transgresses. A deity of many faces, he appears in this sonnet in the guise as the ultimate seducer, Ganymede being one in a long list of conquests.

How do we connect Arguijo's Ganymede, in painting and sonnet, to the symbolic order and the humanist program announced in the inscription "Dedicated to genius and the muses"? How does Ganymede become a fitting companion to Phaëthon in fame and name? And how does he square with the tenor of the times in Counter-Reformation Spain, where nudity was frowned upon? Even Pacheco, who painted an erotic Ganymede in the Duke of Alcala's palace, spoke disapprovingly of nudity, as he wrote in his much-cited *Arte de la pintura* (1622):

> Los famosos pintores, que se han extremado con la licenciosa expresión de tanta diversidad de fábulas; y hecho estudio particular de ellas, con tanta viveza o lascivia, en debuxo y colorido; cuyos cuadros (como vemos)

ocupan los salones y camarines de los grandes señores y príncipes del mundo. Y los tales artífices alcanzan no sólo grandes premios, pero mayor fama y nombre; que yo (séame lícito hablar así) en ninguna manera les envidio tal honra y aprovechamiento. (Pacheco 1956, 1:412)

(Famous painters have gone to extremes with their licentious renditions of a great variety of ancient myths and have made singular study of them, in drawing and colour, with great vividness and lasciviousness. Their paintings (as we see) grace the halls and chambers of the distinguished noblemen and princes of the world. These artists win not only great rewards but greater fame and renown. However, I (if I may speak like this) in no way envy their honour and advantage.)

Leonard Barkan, discussing what he calls "erotic humanism," notes that writers and artists of the Renaissance, in their search for renaming a love that "dares not speak its name," often equated, albeit in ambiguous terms, the love of a book with homoerotic practices, and sodomy with the study of the classics (1991, 66–70). Building on Barkan's argument, Frederick de Armas identifies Arguijo's Ganymede with the embodiment of the "homoerotic humanist passion," with "the power … of humanism, to dare to recuperate ancient notions and practices that would challenge the constrictive dictates of the Counter-Reformation – forbidden practices that range from the erotic to the pictorial; from homosexual desire to the painting of nude and quasi-nude pictures" (2000, 253).The troubled ride of Ganymede to the stars, and of Phaëton to his death, has to do with a humanist enterprise. It is an inspiration to the poets and artists of Arguijo's academy to follow the calling of pagan arts and letters, as he himself had done in poems and paintings.

Arguijo's Academy

Arguijo's mythological ceiling paintings with his verse commentaries would have remained a private undertaking for his personal enjoyment – much like the Duke of Lerma's pleasure and practice of viewing daily the paintings in the royal palaces (see the introduction) – if he had not presented them for their reception by the academy that met in his library. His project illustrates McGann's notion of a text serving as a material social event, a point in time or a moment in space, where "communicative interchanges" are practised (1991, 21). Juan de Mal Lara in the sixteenth century had underscored the importance of the academy as a social occasion for the reception of texts. In "To the readers" of his *Philosophia vulgar*, he writes: "In other countries it is a laudable custom for all learned men to assist someone who is writing, and even to have the authors read their work in the academies formed for this purpose, and for everyone to give their opinions and to say notable things" (cited in Brown 1978, 22).

Mal Lara's academy attracted luminaries like Fernando de Herrera, whose annotated edition of the poems of Garcilaso de la Vega published in Seville in 1580 undoubtedly profited from the academy's collaboration. Francisco Pacheco, whose academy was the most influential among the several academies in Seville, also profited from Mal Lara's. Arguijo's academy, too, had a large following in its brief life (1594–1608) and served as a venue of cultural exchange and networking beyond the royal court. It was what Guy Lazure calls a "site of knowledge," a place "where identities were fashioned, images projected, and textual or social strategies deployed, … [a place] invested with meaning and appropriated for personal and/or collective self-promotion" (2018, 72). It attracted not only Herrera and Pacheco but the likes of Francisco de Medina, who corrected Arguijo's manuscripts, and a host of others who sought Arguijo's patronage. Rodrigo Caro described Arguijo as "no sólo elegantísimo poeta, sino el Apolo de todos los poetas de España" (not only a most elegant poet, but even the Apollo of all the poets of Spain) and someone "[que] les favorecía a todos con excesivos dones y donativos" (who gave most generous gifts to all) (cited in Sánchez 1961, 203–4). Lope de Vega, who appeared frequently at the academy from 1604, called him the "perfecto cortesano" in the *Dragontea* and praised him in other works. He also dedicated several of his poems to Arguijo (Cruz 1995, 83; Sánchez 1961, 205). One of Lope's *rimas* reads:

¿A quién daré mis rimas
y amorosos cuidados […]?
A vos, Mecenas claro,
dulce, divino Orfeo,
clarísimo Museo,
de los ingenios faro. (Blecua 1983, 15–16)

(To whom will I dedicate my rhymes
and amorous cares …?
To you, wise Patron,
sweet, divine Orpheus,
a wisest Musaeus,
the guiding light of great wits.)

We might imagine the members of the academy reading and perhaps even collaborating in the production of Arguijo's poems on Phaëthon and Ganymede, regarded as two of his best. Through the collective reading of the sonnets and viewing of the paintings, his library became the occasion for a shared performance of pagan myths that had been rewritten and reimagined as powerful exemplars of transgression, human and divine. The library was transformed into what Pierre Nora defined as a *lieu de mémoire*, a place where collective memory is created, where recollections are nourished in "spaces, gestures, images, and objects," and where the intimacy of a collective experience persists (1995, 632–3). A "purely material site, like an archive," writes Nora, "becomes a *lieu de mémoire* only if the imagination invests it with a symbolic aura, inasmuch as it becomes 'the object of a ritual'" (639). Arguijo's paintings and sonnets occasioned such a ritual encounter in the intimacy of the academy's gatherings.

The site for enacting a cultural memory is ultimately where Arguijo's fame and name are inscribed, materially in the ceiling through his coat of arms and socially in the academy itself, where his sonnets are read and remembered. If inscription and memory are central to self-promotion, so is voice in the very texts that the poet produces. In the Phaëthon sonnet a celebratory lyric voice redefines his fall through apostrophe as an emblem of fame. In the Ganymede, the poet ventriloquizes Jupiter, lending his voice to the god, who in the form of an eagle addresses his prey. Jonathan Culler has argued that apostrophe suspends real time, placing the apostrophized entity in the present tense of writing. The time of apostrophe is one of "discourse rather than story." The figures of invocation, suggests Culler, "resist being organized into events that can be narrated, for they are inserted in the poem as elements of the event which the poem is attempting to be" (1981, 149). In other words, "the poem itself is to be the happening." Phaëthon and Ganymede ultimately exist in the present tense of the poet's writing: the act of calling forth presence removes the text from elsewhere. Their presence is anchored in voice itself, in the very act of calling, in the poet's word cast as the instrument for his own self-glorification.

Chapter Five

A Mystic and Her Objects

Luisa de Carvajal y Mendoza (1566–1614), aristocrat, mystic, and activist, is a notable figure in the Counter-Reformation tradition of spirituality. Her mystical poetry incorporates the material culture of her time, religious sculptures, paintings, and relics, and the fine objects that surrounded her during her aristocratic upbringing – tapestries, precious stones, and elegant clothing – despite her rejection of its privileges and material trappings. Her religious practices owed as much to Franciscan examples of devotion and a life of penance and poverty as to the Jesuit model of spirituality, which stresses contemplation and meditation on the material. Central to my analysis is how the religious iconography of the Counter-Reformation – paintings and statuary – shapes the ways Carvajal lives and writes her spiritual life in order to construct her identity as penitent, ascetic, and mystic. Since her poetry is entwined with her early experiences, I will take into account events from her memoirs and details from her abundant correspondence.

Two of Carvajal's letters from London, where she was a Catholic missionary, reveal how she was a product of two distinct cultures. In a letter from London dated 17 December 1607, she makes a request of her Madrid companion and long-time friend Inés de la Asunción:

> Las tijeras y husos de el oro me hacen falta, porque acá hubiera creo, sido muy bien recibido; que no hay una persona que sepa ni aun qué es hilar oro, y gastan mucho traído de Italia; y de sólo oír cómo se hila, gustan harto; pienso se vendería bien, y no hallamos labor qué hacer que valga nada ni donde nos la den, como son herejes todos los que tienen tiendas. (Abad 1965, 235)

> (I really need the scissors and spindles for the gold, because here I think they would be very well received, as there is not one person here who

knows how to spin gold, and they spend a lot in bringing it from Italy. Even just hearing how it is spun gives people great pleasure. I think it would sell very well, and we cannot find any work worth mentioning to do or anywhere that will give it to us, because those who have the shops are all heretics.) (Redworth 2012, 1:289–90)

Six months later, on 29 June 1608, Carvajal sent a long letter to Father Joseph Creswell, vice-prefect of the Jesuit College of St. Alban's in Valladolid, informing him of her first arrest and revisiting, somewhat urgently and insistently, her earlier request to Inés:

Y suplico a vuestra merced se acuerde de la necesidad con que estamos yo y mis cuatro compañeras de tener en qué trabajar, para que es necesario tijeras de bordar oro y hilarlo, y acá no se hallan. Y háme escrito mi monja, sor Inés, que ha enviado una caja a vuestra merced con unas muy escogidas, y husos, y otras cosas necesarias. Y si no han venido aún a manos de vuestra merced, vuestra merced me haga merced de escribirla que lo envíe [...]. El oro dicen no se hila aquí; y así, será lo mejor que podremos hacer. Y está todo cada día más caro. (Abad 1965, 249)

(I beg your honour to recall the need that my four companions and I have of finding some work to do. For this we need some embroidery scissors for working with gold and spinning it; and here there are none to be found. My dear nun, Sister Inés, has written to me saying that she has sent you a box, sir, with some quality scissors and spindles, and other necessary things. If they have not yet reached your honour, please be so kind as to write to her to send it ... They say that no one spins gold here, so that this would be the best thing to do. Everything costs more by the day.) (Redworth 2012, 2:7)

The letters tell of the dire circumstances faced by Catholic missionaries in a hostile Jacobean London, but they also reveal how Carvajal, born into the wealthy and powerful Mendoza and Carvajal clans, drew on her knowledge and skills at needlework and at spinning gold thread to support herself and her impoverished companions.[1] These embroidery scissors and spindles are material sites of a cultural and ideological divide. As tools for making luxurious cloth and fine needlework in the private chambers of aristocratic ladies, they were the very symbols of a privileged lifestyle. Here they take on a utilitarian value, however, as Carvajal repurposed them for the production of commercial goods made by manual labour – in effect, luxury items to be brought into the public domain for sale in an urban arena of markets and fairs, merchants and shopkeepers. The project of Carvajal the artisan was shrewd as well as practical, for the market in gold thread was dominated by expensive Italian imports (Jones and Stallybrass 2000, 24–5).

The chronology of Carvajal's life is well known. Orphaned at the age of six, she was sent to Madrid to live at court with her maternal great-aunt María Chacón, governess to the daughters of Philip II, Isabel Clara Eugenia and Catalina Micaela, and to Prince Fernando. For four years Carvajal stayed in the palace of Philip's sister, Juana de Austria (d. 1573), next to the Monasterio de las Descalzas Reales, a convent for noble-born Franciscan nuns, which Juana founded in 1559. There she learned to read and embroider although, as she recalls in her autobiography, she spent most of her time playing with dolls and dress-up with the infantas.[2] After her great-aunt's death in 1576, ten-year-old Luisa was sent to live at palaces in Monteagudo, then Almazán, and finally Pamplona on the viceregal estate of her uncle, Francisco Hurtado de Mendoza, count of Monteagudo, marquis of Almazán, and viceroy of Navarre, who provided her with a fine education and access to his large library (Bouza 1999). Also, by her own account, she was subjected to extreme penitential practices, which indelibly marked her. On her uncle's death in 1586, twenty-year-old Carvajal moved to the Calle de Toledo in Madrid, where for two decades she lived with her servants in abject poverty, begging and doing charitable work, to the embarrassment of her aristocratic relatives.[3] It was during her Madrid period, before she travelled to London as a missionary, that she supposedly wrote her poetry.

The Body of Christ

Carvajal's first poem, a pastoral, "Redondillas espirituales de Silva" (Silva, an anagram for Luisa, was her poetic persona), tells of her encounter with Christ. It was prompted by a question from a shepherdess friend: Why had she "forgotten" her sheep and even herself? In response, Silva explains how she found her shepherd and lover – Christ is here a figure of seductive physical beauty – and became his slave. Carvajal continues a medieval tradition, common in hagiography, whereby female religious emphasize in highly sexual terms a relation with Christ as bridegroom in the form of a "handsome, young, human Christ" (Bynum 1982, 162), the very language of erotic mysticism.[4] Silva's elaborate portrait of Christ relies on a Petrarchan canon of ideal beauty, displaying him as a collection of exquisite objects, body parts as beautiful fetishes to be celebrated and adored.[5] Silva, a mystical celebrant, focuses on Christ's "claros ojos bellos," which made her his prisoner; marks of his divinity, they are brighter than diamonds ("entre su garzo color, / aquellas luces divinas / a las piedras diamantinas / quitaban el resplandor"; 1.53–6, 427).[6] She praises his forehead, his mouth, his teeth, feet, and red lips ("rojo carmesí"; 1.78, 428). Among the fetishes two are not part of the canon – his perfect, chiselled nose ("la nariz afilada / de notable perfección"; 1.69–70, 428) and his brown hair – which are the physical traits of an archetypal Christ found in paintings of the period, like Titian's well-known *Noli me tangere* (1553) and his *Ecce Homo* (fig. 5.1), which hung at the time in the Alcázar; its sexualized figure seemed to play with the enthusiasm of women religious for the handsome Christ. Carvajal reworks the canon's golden-hair motif by making Christ's brown hair the source of the sun's golden rays: "sus castaños cabellos, / que deben ser adorados, / más que aquese sol dorados, / pues su luz recibe dellos" (1.57–60, 428). The most striking body parts and the most significant, given Carvajal's fascination with the meshing of beauty and blood, with its emphasis on vision,[7] are Christ's white hands bearing wounds:

¿Quién jamás hubo mirado
sus manos como la nieve [....]?
En las cuales matizaban
las rubicundas heridas,
y entre lo blanco esculpidas
su lindeza acrecentaban. (1.81–2, 85–8, 428)

(Who has ever looked upon
his snowy white hands ...?
On which were visible
deep red wounds,
which, sculpted on the white marble,
seemed even more beautiful.)

The beauty of the bloody wounds is magnified by being "sculpted" on the white flesh, a sensory experience that accompanies the visual effect. Silva appears to be viewing a painting or, more likely, a polychromatic sculpture of the crucified Christ like those commonly found in churches and monasteries and in the private chapels of the nobility (fig. 5.2).

The poem's seductive fetishes, concrete objects calling attention to their own materiality, affirm Christ's bodily presence, which has a physicality central to the doctrine of the Incarnation, of the divine Word made flesh. The visual rhetoric of fragments recalls the cult of relics, for

Figure 5.1 Titian, *Ecce Homo*, 1547, oil on slate. © Museo Nacional del Prado/Art Resource, New York.

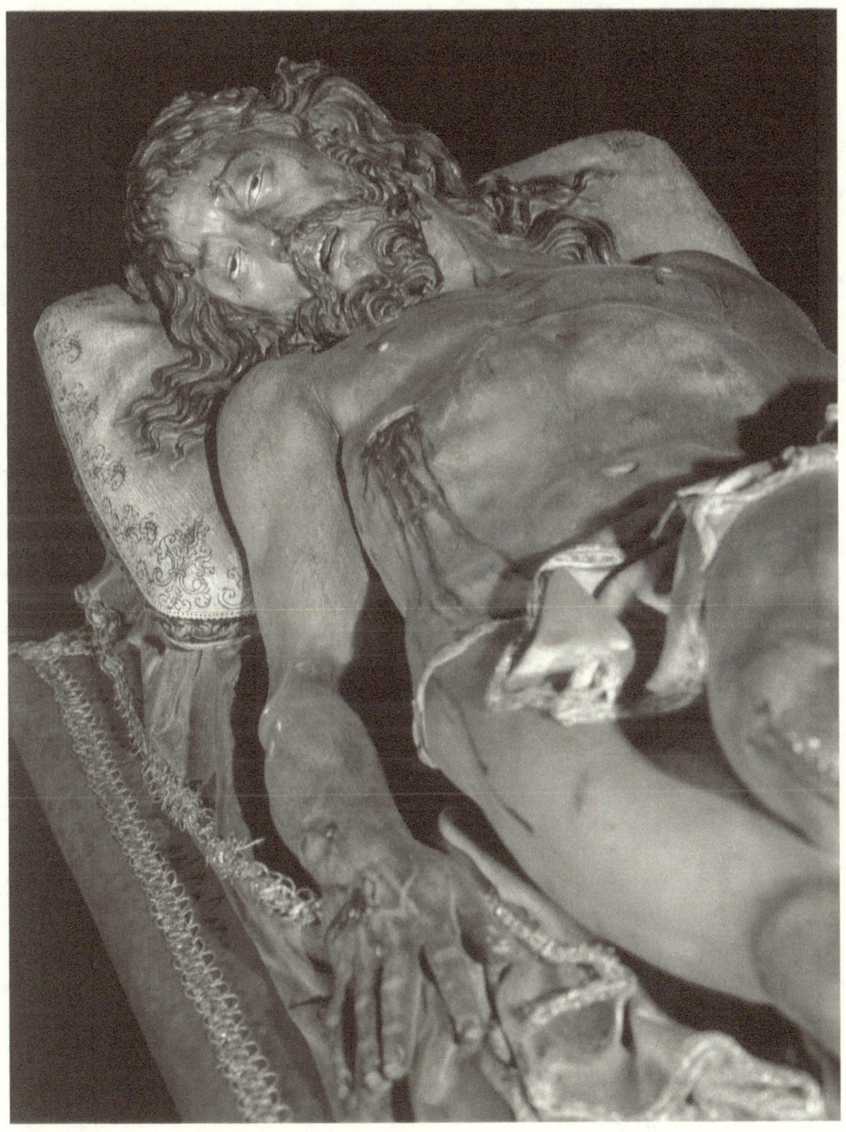

Figure 5.2 Gregorio Fernández, *The Supine Christ*, seventeenth-century, polychromed wood, Convento de los Capuchinos de El Pardo. Album / Art Resource, New York.

Christ's corporeal pieces, the remains of his sacred body, are holy and fit for veneration and healing. It is no coincidence that Silva calls the bodily remains that spiritually enrich her, "despojos":

> La aurora me pareció
> cuando en él puse los ojos,
> que con inmensos *despojos*
> el alma me enriqueció. (1.105–8, 428; my emphasis)
>
> (He seemed to me like a dawn
> when I gazed upon him,
> who with his glorious *remains*
> enriched my soul.)

At once like relics and unlike relics, the remains are parts of a living presence.[8] Commenting on the five wounds of Christ, which in fifteenth-century iconography were often placed on fragments of his body, Bynum writes that "the visual partition of Christ's body is not entirely parallel to relic division. These images insist on Christ's parts as living and bleeding flesh, whereas the form of reliquaries stresses the hardness of bodily remains … Five-wound images stress body parts as alive and bleeding … They show [the body] spilling forth or oozing red, liquid, uncoagulated blood, yet they contain both the part and the bleeding" (2011, 93–4). In Silva's portrait, too, Christ's bodily parts are displayed as living fragments, and Christ's wounds are shown oozing blood ("rubicundas heridas"). Toward the end of Silva's portrait, another wound enters the text with special material significance, the lance wound on Christ's right side, which he himself mentions, his voice echoing in Silva's own:

> Díjome […]
> […………..]
> Y que a tanto había llegado,
> que abrió para entrar en Sí
> *una puerta*, que yo vi
> *rasgada en su diestro lado.* (1.113, 117–20, 428; my emphasis)
>
> (He said to me …
> ………………….
> that he had gone so far
> as to open *a door*, which I saw

ripped open on his right side,
so that I could enter Him.)

The unhealed wound is conceived as a door that Christ opens for Silva, an entryway into his body and a site of redemption. Carvajal's text lies fully within the long-standing devotion to the wound in late medieval and early modern imagery of the Passion. Christ as Saviour plays an active role in this visual tradition, with its strong meditative element, one of the "means of establishing the authority of the message (and the messenger)," but also expressing the desire for intimacy, for a "personal encounter between the human and divine" (Lewis 1997, 209). The wound is the sacred space, the discursive site of the redemptive message of Christ as Saviour, who establishes a dialogue with the viewer: silently as in the psalter of Bonne of Luxembourg, where a crucified Christ stands before Bonne and her husband, Jean of Valois, pointing to his wound with a free right hand (fig. 5.3), or voiced as in the *Passional of Abbess Kunigunde,* where Christ says to her, "*Behold* the grievous wounds and lashes which I have suffered" (cited in Lewis 1997, 212; my emphasis), his words illustrated by an image of a kneeling Kunigunde, her eyes fixed on his lance wound.

Christ's authority and intimacy are evident in Carvajal's text, and Christ the "messenger" and Redeemer is given a voice within this intimate visual field, as he shows his lance wound to Silva. Images of the side wound often appear in medieval religious iconography as a mouth or as a vagina, "the opening from which the salvation of the world was born and into which saved souls return to rest in the center of Christ" (Bynum 2011, 199, note to fig. 45). Carvajal, however, offers an Augustinian interpretation of the wound as a door, which finds its origin in the Gospel of John: "I am the door: by me if any man enter in, he shall be saved: and he shall go in and out, and shall find pastures" (Vulgate, 10:9). Augustine expands the image in the *City of God*: "And the door which was set in the side of [the Ark] clearly represents the wound made in the side of the Crucified when it was pierced with a spear, which is indeed the way of entrance for those who come to Him, because from that wound there flowed the sacraments in which believers are initiated" (1998, 15.26, 687).

Echoing the Augustinian text, Carvajal elaborates the door's sacramental value in "Soneto espiritual de Silva" (number 18), where the divine Word ("divino Verbo") and sweet Lover ("dulce Amado") speak

Figure 5.3 Jean le Noir (fl. 1331–75; attributed to and workshop of), *Crucifixion with Bonne and Jean, Duke of Normandy, Kneeling before the Cross*, before 1349, tempera, grisaille, ink, and gold on vellum. From the *Psalter and Hours of Bonne of Luxembourg*, MS 69.86, fol. 328r, Paris. The Cloisters Collection. © The Metropolitan Museum of Art/Art Resource, New York.

to "the soul" that is receiving the Eucharist, inviting it to enter his chest through the door in his right side. Christ points the way visually to his "sublime majesty"; the dove image from the *Song of Songs* and its redoing in Saint John's *Cántico espiritual* offer the typical tender touch: "y por *la puerta deste diestro lado* / éntrate, palomilla, acá en mi pecho [...] / Mira cómo te entrego, amiga mía, / todo mi ser y *alteza sublimada*" (Juan de la Cruz 2002, 3–4, 9–10, 438, my emphasis; and through the door on my right side, here on my chest, come in, little dove. See how I give you, my friend, all my being and sublime majesty). The "Romance espiritual de Silva" (number 26) goes one step further, furnishing the cultural context that gives special meaning to the wound as a door within Carvajal's poetic production: it is the entrance to Christ's body conceived as the Real Alcázar, the place in which a vulnerable Silva escaped her spiritual troubles ("aprietos") by seeking a mighty refuge ("soberano refugio"):

y, viendo abierta la puerta
al lado del Real Alcázar,
dándole amor osadía,
y prestándole sus alas,
voló hasta dentro del pecho. (26.27–31, 441)

(and standing next to the Royal Alcázar,
seeing its door open,
Love giving her daring,
and lending her his wings,
she flew into his chest.)

Madrid's Alcázar, the royal palace and permanent seat of Philip II's court, had been a Muslim fortress (*al-qasr*) reconstructed by the Habsburgs. The original meaning of *alcázar* did not escape Carvajal. Having lived in Princess Juana's palace next to the sumptuous Descalzas Reales, she surely visited the Alcázar, the locus of power and authority and a place of strength during, in retrospect, the most secure period of her troubled life. She recalled her great-aunt's words when she was about to be taken from the court: "No temáis, hija mía, que nadie os quitará de conmigo, porque no lo consentiré yo" (Abad 1966a, 141; Do not fear, my child, that no one will take you away from me, because I will not permit it). After her aunt's death, when the time came for her to leave, Carvajal wrote, "Deseaba quedar de asiento en palacio" (I wished to stay at court), and added modestly, as if justifying her desire to remain at the palace, "Creo que por desearlo [Isabel de] Ayllón," her governess (142; I believe because Ayllón wanted it). Years later, after she had rejected her aristocratic roots, she carried its material world into the spiritual realm, overlaying her experience and memory of those early years with the interior, protective space that is Christ's chest conceived as the Real Alcázar. Silva defines Christ with the epithet "Real," as in "Real presencia" (Redondillas espirituales, 1.138, 428) and "Real grandeza" (Quintillas espirituales, 5.76, 432), and, following St. Ignatius's name for Christ in his *Spiritual Exercises,* she calls him "majestad." Christ is also a city – "La ciudad soberana / de mi refugio y defensa" (Romance espiritual, 30.18–19, 443; the mighty city of my refuge and defence) – not Augustine's heavenly city ("ni ciudad a la del cielo") but rather Christ's own chest. Once again the lance wound is the door:

[...] tu pecho divino,
adonde nido y morada
me hiciste, abriéndome puerta
con el hierro de una lanza. (30.29–32, 443)

(... your divine chest,
where you built for me
a nest and a home,
opening a door
with the iron of a lance.)

The Divine Maker and His Gifts

In the second part of "Redondillas espirituales" (number 1), Silva gathers Christ's bodily fragments into a whole, a figure spreading a thousand graces ("cien mil gracias derramaba"; 1.129, 428), echoing Saint John's *Cántico espiritual* when the divine lover "mil gracias derramando" passes by the "sotos" (bushes), imprinting them with his divine beauty (Juan de la Cruz 2002, 5.21–5). Christ enters Silva's garden, where nature becomes active and a luxurious, reified *hortus conclusus* reveals its kinship with its maker ("Hacedor"): golden sunflowers turn into fine gold, the greenery clothes itself with joy, carnations and roses are brighter than blood, and the fountain, seeking Christ's presence, stops at his feet as if to render homage. The entrance into the garden, an image of penetration, stands typically for the mystical union.

Carvajal frames Silva's union with Christ in terms of a gift exchange, a vestige from her aristocratic past:

En lugar de arras me dió,
con otras joyas gloriosas,
dos finas piedras preciosas,
y Él el alma me llevó. (1.193–6, 429)

(Instead of a dower, He gave me,
along with other glorious jewels,
two fine precious stones,
and took away my soul.)

"Arras" is the dower, the property or income assigned by the husband to the wife to seal the marriage contract (Covarrubias 1984, 149), providing her with a measure of financial security. Christ seals his union with Silva not with worldly goods associated with an earthly marriage but with other treasures, "joyas gloriosas," pointing to the sacred manifest in the material, that is, Christ himself. Two "finas piedras preciosas" most likely denote his eyes, which earlier in the poem were called "luces divinas" (divine lights) and were brighter than diamonds: "a las piedras diamantinas / quitaban el resplandor" (1.55–6, 427; he robbed the diamond stones of their radiance). Christ takes Silva's soul as her gift to him. In this stanza Carvajal rejects man-made law and a marriage code operative at court and beyond.

Jewels and precious stones were conventional celebratory objects that defined the beauty of the beloved in baroque poetry, as in familiar images by Luis de Góngora and Francisco de Quevedo. Silva's gift exchange, though occurring within a mystical scene, calls to mind a common practice in aristocratic culture. We cannot help but think of the jewels and gems – and of "arras," a tapestry in the terminology of the times – as items of gift-giving on the occasion of weddings, birthdays, or diplomatic events, which a young Carvajal must have witnessed at court. The fact that Silva accepts precious stones from Christ is significant, for within a religious context their beauty and splendour denote and confer sacrality, as in the case of the New Jerusalem described in Revelations: "Having the glory of God [its maker and architect], her light was like a most precious stone, clear as crystal." The city was "pure gold," and "the foundations of its wall" were "adorned with all kinds of precious stones" (Vulgate, 21:18–20). From the Middle Ages onward, reliquaries, crosses, and liturgical objects were equally adorned. Among the many reliquaries in Philip II's possession, one in particular, which had belonged to Charles I and the dukes of Burgundy, bore a gold fleur-de-lis, with a Christ on the cross that was adorned with fine details: three gold and diamond nails accompanied an assortment of designs surrounding the cross, which was encrusted with pearls, rubies, sapphires, diamonds, and emeralds (Sánchez Cantón 1956–9, 10.1.4–6). If Carvajal saw this or similar objects at the Alcázar or at the Descalzas Reales, where the nuns' dowries included luxurious reliquaries and religious objects, she conflated them with her image of Christ's divine presence. Having rejected the precious objects of her aristocratic culture, Carvajal paradoxically made them "live" in Christ, announcing the holy presence of the Word made flesh, just as she imagined Christ as the Real Alcázar, at once a safe refuge and the king's palace and repository of royal treasures.

Christ at the Column

Carvajal devotes two poems, "Redondillas espirituales de Silva" (number 24) and "Quintillas espirituales de Silva" (number 25), to another material object of Christological significance, the foot in an image of Christ at the column, in which a bleeding Christ, ropes around his wrists and tied to a column, has been scourged. This was a popular subject in works of art of the period, notably in polychromatic sculptures like the one by Gregorio Fernández, which now stands at the Real Monasterio de la Encarnación in Madrid (fig. 5.4). In her prose introduction to the "Redondillas," Carvajal mentions Christ at the column with an image focused on the foot: "A Cristo Nuestro Señor, sobre su divino pie izquierdo, el cual se mostraba en una imagen de la columna, de ella amarrado" (To Christ Our Lord, on his divine left foot, in an image of the column to which he is tied). The sculpted foot is an ideal material site to examine the dynamic of the mystic subject's dialogue with Christ, a rhetoric of meditation linked to the look and to Carvajal's life events, specifically to her discipline and flagellation at the hands of her uncle's servants in Pamplona. This is a devotional poem of Silva's re-enactment of a visual memory as she stood in front of the image, addressing Christ and visualizing a concrete part of his body. The specular dimension is evident from the start: "El pie que de amor me hirió / de sólo mirarle un día" (24.1–2, 440; the foot that wounded me with love / as I gazed upon it one day). Prayer and meditation on the images of Christ – as Ignatius of Loyola had prescribed – had the most effect on Carvajal's devotion, as she writes in her autobiography: "El mirar de las imágenes de Cristo nuestro Señor, aunque fuese de paso, todo venía a parar en revertírseme allá en lo íntimo del alma un afecto de amor terrible y de desear seguir su fragoso camino hasta la

Figure 5.4 Gregorio Fernández, *Christ at the Column*, Real Monasterio de la Encarnación, Madrid. Album/Art Resource, New York.

muerte" (Abad 1966a, 194; In my looking at the images of Christ, our Lord, even for a moment, all came to rest in the most intimate place in my soul, awakening in me a huge love and a desire to follow his rough journey until death). Carvajal was adept at the Ignatian style of spiritual meditation, perhaps having practised it during her days at the Descalzas Reales, where the Jesuit Superior General Francisco de Borja was extremely influential. She also practised it fully at Pamplona under the supervision of her uncle, who had been instructed by Borja himself (1966, 151n3, 152).[9]

Carvajal meditated often on Christ's "derramamientos de sangre" (the shedding of blood), one of which was the flagellation at the column.[10] Despite the poem's prefatory words alerting the reader to the image of Christ at the column, one of the instruments of his Passion (*arma Christi*), the text is not about flagellation. Yet the choice of a suffering Christ, covered with blood, is the site for Luisa's dramatic act of humility and a mystical experience with overtones of Franciscan spirituality:

El pie tu Silva besando
que juntamente adoraba,
dél sentí que al alma entraba
un fuego y otro abrasando.
Y abierto hasta el corazón
el camino a puro fuego,
a paso llano el pie luego
entró a tomar posesión.
Y tan perdida quedé,
cuando los ojos, por verle,
alcé, que, por no perderle,
me di, por el dulce pie.
[............................]
Aquesto así ejecutado,
me fuera suma riqueza
verle sobre mi cabeza
después de haberle besado. (24.13–24, 29–32, 440)

(As your Silva kissed your foot,
which she intimately adored,
I felt from it a fire and, yet another,
entering and burning my soul.
And the way to my heart

opened by pure fire,
your foot then, slowly but surely,
entered to take possession.
And I so lost myself,
when I raised my eyes to see it,
that, so as not to lose
sight of it, I surrendered to the sweet foot.
....
This having been done,
it would be a source of great riches,
to see it now on my head
after having kissed it.)

The two key moments, the kissing of the foot and the wish to have that foot lie on her head, echo Christian texts, iconography, and practices. The gesture of Mary Magdalene washing Christ's feet with her tears, wiping them with her hair, and kissing and anointing them is iconic (Luke 7:36–8). So are the images of Saint Francis of Assisi, who having taken vows of obedience and humility, appears in numerous paintings, kissing Christ's feet, making for a cult-like reverence to the saint and his followers. In her autobiography Carvajal writes that she took to charity work at an early age in imitation of her mother or to please her, and when the discalced Franciscan friars, to whom her mother was especially devoted, visited the house, she would kneel and kiss their feet ("me ponía a sus pies y se los besaba"; Abad 1966a, 132). Her mother's devotion to Saint Francis extended to domestic practices in their home, where a young Luisa would dress at times in a Franciscan-style habit that was embroidered in the finest brown silk (133).

The foot is the instrument of Silva's mystical journey, the trigger of the trance ("tan perdida quedé") that causes the erotic and spiritual fire that burns her soul and carves the way for it to enter her heart. Saint John in his *Cántico espiritual* wishes Christ's eyes to be drawn ("dibujados") within, in his bowels ("entrañas") in a specular play with the fountain waters (Juan de la Cruz 2002, 11.51–5). Silva, for her part, places Christ's foot, adored and venerated, within her. Still in her trance, she looks up at the sculpted Christ and sees the "dulce pie." Later, she refers to the "painted foot," hinting at a polychromatic flagellated Christ with his foot painted red, oozing blood, which she wants to be placed on her head as a source of spiritual riches ("suma riqueza"). Silva turns into an erotic and mystical event the militant images in the standard iconography of a triumphant Christ treading on animals, in Psalm 90 ("Thou shalt walk upon the asp and the basilisk; and thou shalt trample underfoot the lion and the dragon"; Vulgate 90:13), and warrior figures, slayers of dragons like St. Michael. The triumphant Christ ("vencedor") conquers her not only with his right arm but with his left foot, which inflicts the wound that "kills" her with love.

Carvajal's autobiography resonates in the poem, where she transforms her earlier violent mortification into a loving union with Christ. She recounts the flagellations intended to teach her "perfect obedience" and to "break her will" (Abad 1966a, 161). Although her uncle initiates her gently into self-flagellation, giving her a "disciplina" made out of delicate white silk, the eager Luisa, finding it too soft, ties to it "a silver thistle" (152–3). Self-flagellation, however, did not compare with the brutal whipping that her uncle's servants were instructed to inflict on her. She tells how, stripped of her clothing, she was disciplined by a servant:

> Ella llegaba con unas disciplinas de cuerdas de vigüelas nada blandas, y me disciplinaba el tiempo que le parecía con golpes tan bien dados, que apenas los podía algunas veces sufrir [...] Y acabada la disciplina, muchas veces me mandaba con mucho señorío, que le besase los pies; y yo, postrada en el suelo, se los besaba. (Abad 1966a, 162, 181–2)

> (She arrived with a few disciplines made of vihuela cords not at all soft, and she disciplined me as long as she wished with blows so well placed that I could hardly stand it ... And the discipline finished, she commanded me many times with much arrogance to kiss her feet; and I, lying on the floor, would kiss them.)

On another occasion, she is tied to a column and scourged, with echoes of *Cristo a la columna*:

> Cuando se resolvía en que la disciplina fuese de los pies a la cabeza, con una toalla puesta por la cinta de la manera que se pinta un crucifijo, y atada a una columna que para eso había hecha a propósito; y los pies en la tierra fría, y una soga de cáñamo a la garganta, con cuyos cabos se ataban las muñecas y manos a la columna. (Abad 1966a, 182)

> (When it was decided that the discipline would be from head to toe, a towel was placed around my waist as seen on a crucifix, and tied to a column that she made for this purpose; my feet on the cold floor, and a

hemp cord on my throat, with both ends tying my wrists and hands to the column.)

And again, after Carvajal, with rope tied around her neck and hands, had been whipped by the servant:

> Me puso uno de sus pies sobre el pecho, en medio dél. Y como tenía un zapato de dos suelas, grosero, y debió descuidarse en cargar demasiado, sentí grande pena dentro del pecho y en todo lo interior dél. (Abad 1966a, 185)
>
> (She put one of her feet on the middle of my chest. And as her shoe was thick, with double soles, and pressing it without much thought and with great force, I felt a great pain inside my chest.)

Whether these accounts are real or imagined or are life events combined with details from hagiographic stories or religious writers like Luis de Granada – several of his books were in her uncle's library – we will never know.[11] Yet, the scourging at the column, the kissing of the feet, the stepping on the body in her autobiographical recollections are articulated in her poem as part of an intimate mystical performance, a self-conscious staging that would eventually find its way into print.

Last Will and Testament

Anticipating her death from the love wound inflicted by Christ, Silva writes her last will and testament, disposing of all her possessions ("Romance espiritual del testamento de Silva," number 6). She sends her soul to the Shepherd, who branded her body with an intertwined S and nail, the mark of the slave and a symbol of obedience and humility, a well-known practice of the time when slaves were branded in this way on the face and body (Carvajal y Mendoza 1990, 76n15). Imprinted with this "precept," which also appears in poem 31, her body promises humbly to obey her soul, "su señora" (her mistress). We know that Carvajal left her inheritance to the Jesuit English Mission for the founding of a novitiate, which was eventually built in Louvain (Abad 1966b, 383). Here Silva leaves her imagined personal possessions to the nobles at court, mocking their frivolous lifestyle. To the avaricious rich ("ricos avaros"), Silva leaves the gold of the Tiber; to lords and grandees, she bequeaths a mountain of vanity, and to the ladies she gives her fancy clothes and trinkets:

Las galas manda a las damas:
y toda la bizarría,
guantes, ámbar y pebetes,
cazoletas y pastillas,
fiestas, banquetes, jardines,
faustos, pompas, cortesías. (6.41–6, 432–3)[12]

(Fancy clothes she sends to the ladies:
and all the trinkets and ornaments,
gloves, amber and incense,
perfumes and aromatic pills,
parties, banquets, gardens,
luxuries, pomp, social graces.)

By giving away these luxury items along with a carefree life of banquets and pomp, signs of aristocratic ease and splendour (all that constitute the "estamento nobilario"), Silva breaches a class divide, breaking the social code of a society in which prestige and status depended on class ("sociedad estamental").[13] Carvajal already had transgressed the code of honour when she moved to Madrid's Calle de Toledo, taking with her only the bare necessities. She writes about the danger: "Volviendo las espaldas a todo me puse en el modo que deseaba en medio de lo más florido de la edad y de la corte de España donde forzosamente me hallaba y con un enemigo poderoso de desordenada afición al resplandor y honra mundana" (cited in Pinillos 2001, 56; Turning my back to everything, I became all that I wanted to be, at the centre of the most exclusive society and the Habsburg court, where I inevitably found myself against a powerful enemy of an unruly penchant for splendour and worldly fame). Wearing ragged clothing and living in dire poverty, she earned the scorn of her family. She became "a holy woman," establishing a kind of counter-court in her house, a *beaterio*, "a community of single women who devoted themselves to the ideals of the primitive Christian church while living in the world" (Rhodes 2000, 9). Her transgressive performance flowed from her sense of entitlement. If the poem speaks of Silva's rejection of her noble status and her severing of all ties with the aristocratic community, the real Luisa, though tending to the poor and prostitutes (according to her companion Inés de la Asunción), also received friends from the nobility in her home, often patrons of the Jesuits "para consolarse y tratar de sus necesidades espirituales y tomar consejo" (Abad 1966a, 75; in order to console herself, treat her spiritual needs, and get advice). She also visited members of the aristocracy, including Queen Margaret and the Infanta Isabel Clara Eugenia.

After her death, Silva leaves her soul in the hands of Christ, who places it in a tomb inside his chest, in place of the earthly tomb built for her. As with the image of Christ as the Real Alcázar, she enters a place of peace and refuge:

> en un glorioso sepulcro
> que dentro en su pecho había,
> dejando el de sumo olvido
> que para Silva tenía
> el vano mundo engañoso
> edificado a gran prisa (6.77–82, 433)
>
> (in a glorious tomb
> inside his chest,
> leaving behind the one worthy of being forgotten,
> which the deceitful world
> had built for Silva
> in a big rush.)

Mystical union is conceived as a burial. Christ's chest becomes the site of a funerary monument, where the Shepherd, "muerto de amores" (dying of love), author and authority of Silva's life and life after death, inscribes an epitaph to preserve her memory securely and privately:

> una letra soberana
> que su memoria eterniza,
> que dice: "Silva, cual Fénix,
> en mil llamas encendida,
> yace dichosa y feliz
> en mí, del mundo escondida." (6.85–90, 433)
>
> (a majestic inscription
> that perpetuates her memory,
> which reads "Silva, like a Phoenix,
> burning with a thousand flames,
> lies happy and blissful,
> inside of me, hidden from the world.")

Figure 5.5 Francisco Giralte, interior of the Capilla del Obispo, Madrid. Album / Art Resource, New York.

Christ's voice frames, stages, and defines Silva's sacred space inside him, where saved souls traditionally return to rest. The epitaph is an inscription written by Christ, the Word made flesh, on the durable surface of her tomb. Bound by the language and iconography that have been fashioned for him by tradition, Christ bestows on Silva the Phoenix, the very symbol of his resurrection. Dying to the world, Silva is resurrected in a specular image that further emphasizes their union as mystical lovers. In Carvajal's poems, Christ is configured in layers, his body as the Alcázar, his side wound conceived as its door, and here her tomb safe within the corporeal fortress.

In placing Silva's tomb with its inscribed epitaph within Christ's body, Carvajal implicitly rivals her paternal grandfather, the bishop of Plasencia, Gutierre de Vargas Carvajal (1506–59). Builder of churches and patron of the arts, he built a magnificent tomb, located in a chapel (called to this day "Capilla del Obispo") next to his palace in Madrid, to memorialize himself and his lineage (fig. 5.5). It was a grandiose affair, which included the alabaster tombs of his parents. A luxurious plateresque retable sculpted by Francisco Giralte, disciple of Berruguete, is flanked by kneeling figures of his father and mother. Gutierre's own kneeling figure – accompanied by those of his secretary, a chaplain, the chapel's sexton, and a cortège of acolytes and holy figures – appears on a wall at the right (Vasallo Toranzo and Pérez Martín 2013, 283). At the back of these figures is a relief of Christ praying in the Garden of Gethsemane. Carvajal does one better: in her poem Christ himself is Silva's tomb and the author of an epitaph, honouring her with his body.

Carvajal's religious poetry, written in Madrid after she had rejected the trappings of her aristocratic upbringing, was embedded with material traces of that aristocratic culture as well as of her personal religious experiences. Those material presences occur in reference to the paintings and polychromatic sculptures that she likely viewed, as well as to other objects that functioned as sites of her poetic discourse: precious stones, the Alcázar, her tomb, and numerous depictions of Christ's body, both whole and in parts. Just as Carvajal repurposed the instruments and cloth-work of polite society into tools for the production of commercial goods, so she refashioned the memory of her earlier flagellations, veritable imitations of Christ's Passion, into a triumphant mystical union. The body of Christ becomes her refuge and Alcázar, and his lance wound an entryway into his body, ultimately for her tomb within him. Carvajal's physical humiliations, processed through Ignatian meditation, fuse in her poetry to yield a Franciscan-like mysticism but with culturally specific components: religious artefacts and the material vestiges of her earlier privileged life. It is her reference to those concrete objects that most distinctly marks her poems as material lyric.

Epilogue

In *Shakespeare and Material Culture*, Catherine Richardson (2011) examines "the way early modern men and women used objects, and the way writing and material culture were related to one another in the period in which Shakespeare was producing his plays" (3). In the England of Shakespeare, objects spoke not only through their materiality of shape and function but also through words inscribed on their surfaces. So it was in contemporary Spain, where poets made the material repositories of memory – books, tombs, sculptures – "speak" their embedded knowledge to readers and viewers, who responded by bringing their own learning and cultural practices to bear on what they heard and saw for a fruitful exchange with the object. Visual scenes, too, whether portraits or mythological paintings restaged through the lens of the early modern humanist imagination, spoke figuratively to discerning viewers. In each case, the object, viewer, and lyric text engage in a dynamic cultural performance.

The relation between the self and the object it encounters is explored in *Subject and Object in Renaissance Culture* by Margaret de Grazia, Maureen Quilligan, and Peter Stallybrass (1996), who abandon the notion of Burkhardt's autonomous subject in order to focus on how objects leave their imprint on subjects, who are thereby constituted by them and who in turn own, use, and transform the objects. They conclude, in short, that "what we have to gain in interrelating the object and the subject ... is a sense of how objects have a hold on subjects as well as subjects on objects" (11). *A Poetry of Things* explores that dynamic and extends it by ascribing agency to objects that not only speak but assume human characteristics and display their own subjectivity, as in Quevedo's *túmulos*, where the wood fragment from Columbus's ship, which was buried with him in his tomb, asserts itself by telling an intimate story of its own life to passers-by, and where the marble of

Osuna's tomb claims authorship of its epitaph by declaring "I am memory." In Carvajal a living Christ in a polychrome statue speaks to her and inscribes an epitaph on her tomb deep within his body. They illustrate, in their distinctive ways, what Arjun Appadurai calls "the social life of things," in which objects have "life histories" or "careers" determined by their production and circulation, and so they are invested with social significance and cultural values (1986, 34, 41–2). If some objects speak, others elicit visual or textual memories that initiate dialogic exchanges. Objects assuming agency act as if they inhabited the same experiential world as their subjects.

Vision and visuality are strongly embedded in the texts studied here. As viewers interact with and project meaning onto objects, the objects "look" back to constitute the viewers. When, in *Roman Eyes: Visuality and Subjectivity in Art and Text* (2007), Jaś Elsner comments on Browning's "Rhyme for a Child Viewing a Naked Venus in a Painting for the Judgement of Paris" – "He gazed and gazed and gazed and gazed, / Amazed, amazed, amazed, amazed" – he captures a simple but revealing encounter between a viewer and an object. When we turn to the gaze, he writes, "we move from the material and the objective [...] into a realm of impression, fantasy, and creativity," to investments on subjectivity both collective and individual (xi), a notion that raises fundamental questions about the subjective relations between objects and viewers. When Quevedo as lyric subject enters the Capitoline Museum, he transforms the inanimate objects caught in his own amazement: for him, Marcus Aurelius in bronze is actually there, "flying" on his "armed horse." Carvajal too, through her gaze, animates a mute sculpture of Christ, who speaks and writes.

Formulations that define place and space as active zones of human experience have enriched my reading of the material lyric. Michel de Certeau's concept of space as a "practiced place" activated by "walkers" resonates, most significantly, with the pilgrims and passers-by who activate the scripted memory of tombstones, and with the "actors" who pass through the liminal space of the seashore in Góngora's *Polifemo*. Henri Lefebvre's concept of space as something "produced" by social relations in everyday experience complements de Certeau's formulation. The interactive landscapes of the *Polifemo* are produced by social and cultural activities like hunting, storytelling, gift-giving, and courtship. The learned members of Arguijo's academy, who interact in his library with his mythological ceiling paintings and sonnet-commentaries, produce a space of cultural memory and knowledge. Quevedo, too, produces a space of cultural memory and knowledge by reading his learned books in his retreat in la Torre de Juan Abad – presumably with the aid of mechanical devices (a turnstile to read several books at once, and a table on wheels to read in bed). For her part, Carvajal produces an imagined sacred space by dialoguing with a Christ in canvas and wood through vision and meditation.

The material lyric in Spain, as in Shakespeare's England, reflected the profusion of cultural objects at a time when the production, circulation, collection, and display of objects of diverse provenance filled public and private spaces, demanding recognition in their own right within the sphere of human affairs. Quevedo, Góngora, Arguijo, and Carvajal inhabited the same realm of the material and shared the same fascination with objects as did the Duke of Lerma, who took pleasure, as Rubens remarked approvingly in 1603, in viewing daily the paintings hanging in the royal palace. His ritual practice was in a larger sense a pilgrimage in search of knowledge embedded in the displayed objects. The poets in this study pursued comparable "conversations" with objects, as they interrogated image and script in order to access memory and history. The material lyric was an ideal vehicle for their cultural explorations.[1]

Notes

Introduction

1 In Lefebvre's triad, "perceived space" and "lived space" are accompanied by "conceived space," expressed in "numbers" and "verbal signs" in the grids and maps of social engineers, architects, and urban planners ([1974] 1991, 38–9). I use W.J.T. Mitchell's concept of landscape, a scene mediated by culture and a medium of exchange, to analyse the *locus amoenus* in Góngora's *Polifemo* as a dynamic space (see chapter 3).

2 Tuan, a human geographer, conceives place and space as "modes of experience" – tactile, visual, conceptual – and "as images of complex [...] feelings" (1977, 3), hence his interest in Bohr's and Heisenberg's reactions when they visit Kronberg. For a study that applies Tuan's theory of place and space to the uses of architecture in Cervantes's *Persiles* IV, see Frederick de Armas (2019). María Cristina Quintero studies place and space in panegyric sonnets by Góngora, where she combines de Certeau, W.J.T. Mitchell, and Michel Foucault's heterotopia to examine questions of patronage and power (2016).

3 Francisco de Herrera y Maldonado, a disciple of Lope de Vega, who witnessed the wedding festivities, writes glowingly:

Fue el acompañamiento mayor, más costoso, y lucido, vistoso, y rico que han visto muchos siglos en casamientos de Reyes; las galas, oro, diamantes, perlas, y piedras, de que todos iban cubiertos, no fácil puede decirse: irían seiscientos caballeros, con riquísimas libreas en innumerables pajes, y lacayos, criados, y confidentes.

(It was the largest, most costly, splendid, dazzling, and rich royal wedding that the ages have seen: the costumes, gold, diamonds, pearls, gems that covered the participants defy my description. There must have been 600 gentlemen who rode with innumerable pages, lackeys, servants, and confidants, who themselves wore incredibly rich liveries.)

Libro de la vida y maravillosas virtudes del Siervo de Dios Bernardino de Obregón, Madrid, 1634, fol. 211r (cited in Wright 2001, 52). For the entry of Margaret of Austria into Madrid during the wedding festivities, see Tovar Martín (1988).

4 For this style of portraiture, see Schroth and Baer (2008, 197–201).

5 For an exhaustive study of Maximilian's use of illustrated texts, medals, military artefacts, and even a tomb monument for his "marketing," see Silver (2008).

6 Images of Roman emperors in prints, paintings, and sculptures were popular among the favourites of the Habsburg kings, especially Lerma, who commissioned Vicente Carducho to paint heads of emperors, a total of 153 works (Schroth and Baer 2008, 198–200; 339n15). For his part, to convey his image of royal authority and power, Philip commissioned an equestrian statue cast by the Flemish sculptor Giambologna (Jean Boulogne) and finished by Pietro Tacca in Florence before it was sent to Spain, sometime after 1614. It was placed at the Casa de Campo in Madrid and moved in 1848 to the city's Plaza Mayor, where it still stands.

7 On academies in Spain see, in particular, Brown (1978), Cruz (1995), Egido (1990), King (1960; 1963), and Sánchez (1961).

8 For details, see Elliott ([1963] 2002) and Allen (2000). Allen proposes that Philip III had an ulterior motive for the Pax Hispanica: "The idea was to proffer the laurels of peace to your opponents and persuade them to abandon their military pursuits for a time, while simultaneously maintaining your own military establishment, thereby weakening them seriously in the event of a future engagement" (ix).

9 On the Spain of Philip III and his *valido*, the Duke of Lerma, see in particular Feros (2000, 2002, 2008), Williams (2006), and Allen (2000).

10 For the most comprehensive biography of Quevedo, see Jauralde Pou (1999).

11 On biographical details, see Alonso ([1967] 1994, 31–63) and Bass (2008b, 173–7), with bibliography.

12 For Arguijo's biography, see Vranich (1985, 13–28).

13 For biographical details on Carvajal, see Abad (1966b), Cruz (2014), Rhodes (2000), and Redworth (2008).

14 Unless otherwise noted, translations are my own.

1. The Agency of Objects

1 Quotations from the poems are from Blecua (1969). For the sonnets, volume is followed by page number. For the *silva* "Al pincel," volume is followed by page and line number. I have benefited from translations by Christopher Johnson (2009) to which I have made silent emendations. The translation of sonnet epitaph "Memoria soy del más glorioso pecho" is mine.

2 Tarsia employs the term *museo* as synonymous with a collection. The *Diccionario de Autoridades* defines *museo* as a Wunderkammer: "el lugar en que se guardan varias curiosidades, pertenecientes a las ciencias [conocimiento]: como algunos artificios mathemáticos, pinturas extraordinarias, medallas antiguas" (the place where are kept many curiosities, belonging to the sciences [knowledge]: like mathematical artefacts, extraordinary paintings, ancient medals). Tarsia extends the term *museo* to a collection of books, learned artefacts, with *curiosos* leading to the notion of "cabinet of curiosities," to which Quevedo's books in their diversity implicitly belong. *Museo*, from the Latin *museum* and the Greek *moyseîon*, is a place dedicated to the muses and by extension to the place where literary arts are practised.

3 James Crosby dates this sonnet to 1637 (1967, 171), as he takes into account Quevedo's first editor, who writes in his volume, "Algunos años antes de su prisión última, me envió este excelente soneto desde la Torre [de JuanAbad]" (Quevedo 1648, 115; Some years before his last imprisonment he sent me this excellent sonnet from la Torre de Juan Abad). See, in addition to Crosby, Villanueva (2007), Carreira (1997), López Grigera (1987), Bell (1984), and Rey (1997, 206–8).

4 In one of his epistles in "Epístolas a imitación de las de Seneca" (Epistles in imitation of those by Seneca), Quevedo writes in reference to his exile in la Torre de Juan Abad: "En mi tengo compañía [...] razonan conmigo los libros, cuyas palabras oigo con los ojos" (I have company [...] books speak to me, books whose words I listen to with my eyes; Crosby 1994,179). On redactions of the sonnet, see Crosby (1967, 26–7, 40–1).

5 On Seneca's letters to Lucilius, the *Epistulae morales*, see Edwards (2015, 41–53).

6 For Ficino and Petrarch, I am indebted to Coffin (1979, 9, 12–13).

7 On Quevedo's debt to the *Greek Anthology* see, in particular, Crosby (1966). On tomb epigrams, see Bergmann (1979, 132–65), who includes Quevedo's "El Escarmiento" and sonnets to the tombs of Federico Spínola, Doña Catalina de la Cerda, and Don Berenguel de Aois. See also Ter Horst (2013, 183–4), who cites Tullius Laureas's Sappho epitaph.

8 This subtitle appears in González de Salas's edition (Quevedo 1648).
9 *Libro de las profecías* is a compilation of biblical texts and *auctoritates* (patristic writings, medieval theologians, and canonists). It was designed to locate the discovery of the Indies within the story of salvation, a first step toward the liberation of the Holy Land from Muslim domination. Given that Columbus came back in chains to Spain after his third voyage, the purpose of this volume was to assign himself a prominent role in these events. On the messianic aspects of Columbus's discovery of the Indies, see Zamora (1993, 97) and Milhou (1983).
10 Columbus died in Valladolid in 1506 and was buried there. His remains were then moved to the Carthusian monastery of Santa María de las Cuevas in Seville. In 1542 they were taken to colonial Santo Domingo, where they remained until they were moved to Havana, Cuba, in 1795 after the French had taken over the island of Hispaniola. After the Spanish-American war in 1898, his remains were returned to Spain and now allegedly rest in a tomb in Seville Cathedral.
11 Osuna's real tomb is part of the ducal pantheon in the Collegiate Church of Santa María de la Asunción in Osuna, where the dukes of Osuna and family members are buried.
12 The Pax Hispanica lasted twenty-three years (1598–1621), during which Spain gradually withdrew from the European religious wars. Peace with France, England, and the Netherlands was, however, a political strategy on the part of Philip III. On the Pax Hispanica, see also Elliott ([1963] 2002).
13 On Quevedo and the conspiracy against Venice, see in particular Jauralde Pou (1999, 373–84), Crosby (1955), and Martinengo (1982).
14 In his other sonnet epitaphs Quevedo is equally intense in his praise: "Inscripción en el túmulo de don Pedro Girón, duque de Osuna, virrey y capitán general de las dos Sicilias" – "De la Asia fue terror, de Europa espanto" (He was Asia's terror, Europe's dread) – mentions the duke's military triumphs, along with his trial and his death in prison; and "Compendio de las hazañas del mismo en i[n]cripción sepulcral" – "Diez galeras tomó, treinta bajeles" (He took ten galleons, thirty ships) – celebrates his victories in land and sea. Quevedo admired men of action like Osuna and Fadrique de Toledo, who also fell out of favour and was denied a funeral worthy of his rank and prestige (Jauralde Pou 1999, 678). The sonnet epitaph for Fadrique after his death in 1634, "Venerable túmulo de don Fadrique de Toledo" – "Al bastón que le vistes en la mano" (To the cane that you saw in his hand) – is another example of the poet's defence of a friend and hero, and the injustice to which he had been subjected.

15 Painters had a personal investment in these quarrels beyond the theoretical and the ideological. Jean Hagstrum writes: "[Painters] were now successful enough to reject the inferior social and educational position they had occupied since antiquity and to strive for recognition of their pursuits as liberal disciplines" ([1958] 1987, 66). Quevedo's homage to the art of painting, in its rivalry with nature, may have been prompted by his support of painters in their litigations in Madrid against the Hacienda del Reino, which demanded that painters pay the same taxes that were assessed on artisans and merchants (López Grigera 1975, 225). For details on these litigations see also Candelas Colodrón (1996), who posits that Quevedo's homage also has to do with views of art as an instrument of Counter-Reformation dogmas. For a critical edition on the painters' litigations in their "Memorial informatorio" (1629), see Sánchez Jiménez and Sáez (2018). Laura Bass (2017) studies the *paragone* between poetry and painting from a political perspective, centring on Góngora's rivalry in "Hurtas mi bulto," which contrasts with Quevedo's support of painting in "Al pincel."

16 On the vast literature on illusionism and deception in the treatises of the period and classical predecessors see Hagstrum ([1958] 1987, 23–5, 81–2) and, within the Spanish context, Bergmann (1979, 74–81 and passim). On the foundational *De pictura* by Leon Battista Alberti, see in particular Grafton (2002). Rodrigo Cacho Casal explores the theoretical underpinnings of classical and contemporary art treatises in "Al pincel" (2012a, 89–127), including excerpts from its several redactions. On the chronology and variants of these redactions see Cacho Casal (2012b). For a study of painting in Quevedo's poetry, including "Al pincel," see Sáez (2015).

17 Titian's painting, as mysterious as Rosa herself, is impossible to locate. In a letter dated 11 October 1552 Titian wrote to Philip II, one of his most enthusiastic patrons, that he was sending a portrait of the "Queen of Persia." Two months later Philip replied that the painting had not arrived. On 3 August 1559 the secretary of the Spanish ambassador to Venice, García Hernández, wrote to Philip that he would be sending a small picture by Titian of "una Turca o Persiana hecho [*sic*] a su fantasía" (a Turkish or Persian woman made from his imagination). Apparently neither painting was received, as neither appears in the royal inventories (Cloulas 1967, 215–16; in Wethey 1971, 205). On the many copies of Rosa's portraits in Spain, see Cacho Casal (2012a, 106).

18 Other details, like the colour of her hair and the red hair of the marten, also point to her name (de Armas 1996, 199, and Cacho Casal 2012a, 106).

19 The Venetian diarist Marino Sanuto recorded on 13 March 1532 that he had seen a helmet at the jewellers' district of the Rialto "surmounted by a plume in an elaborate crescent-shaped mount, at whose center was an enormous turquoise surrounded by rubies, diamonds, pearls and emeralds; its headband was studded with pointed diamonds … [and] four removable crowns encircled the helmet; each of the four crown's twelve points was topped with an enormous pearl; in addition the three larger crowns were each set with four diamonds, four rubies, four emeralds" (Jardine 1996, 379).

20 The iconography of the crown, an artefact manufactured by Western goldsmiths, add Jardine and Brotton, "whose cultural and political worth will be equally recognized to both East and West," was "carefully chosen to conform to visual idioms of imperial might in the West; re-circulating westward, it provided an image of an "oriental power figure" (2000, 42).

21 On the *Hypnerotomachia*'s importance to the "reinvention of Egypt" in the Renaissance, see Curran (2007, 133–64). On hieroglyphs in the European tradition see Iversen (1993) and Wittkower (1997). On obelisks and hieroglyphs, see Curran et al. (2009).

22 See Yates [1964] 1977, 163. For Ficino in Spanish letters, see Byrne (2015), with bibliography, and in Quevedo, see Schwartz (1995).

23 On the notions of *Deus artifex* and *Deus pictor* in theoretical and literary works in Spain see Bergmann (1979, 17–71). On the *Deus pictor* in "Al pincel," see Cacho Casal (2012a, 123–7), who cites Carducho, Federico Zuccaro's emblem on painting (*Hinc omnia*), and *Autoridades*.

2. Material Rome

1 Quevedo carried a message to the pope from the Duke of Osuna, urging support for a naval war against Venice. The pope's response, written after his meeting with Quevedo, includes words of praise for the poet as a "caballero de muchas partes, muy entendido, y muy privado del virrey de Nápoles" (cited in Gutiérrez 2005, 221; a well-travelled gentleman, very knowledgeable, and a favourite of the Viceroy of Naples). On the duke's naval campaign, see chapter 1.

2 On the *silva* and Quevedo's in particular, see Rocha de Sigler (1994, 43–117). See also Asensio (1983), Candelas Colodrón (1995, 1997), Jauralde Pou (1991), and Kallendorf and Kallendorf (2000).

3 Cacho Casal, in the Spanish version of his study of the silva (2012a; English version 2009), mentions parts of Freud's passage quoted here and relates it to artificial memory. My interpretation takes a different trajectory.

4 Quotations from Quevedo's *silva* are from Blecua (1969), volume and page followed by line number. I have consulted Kallendorf (2011) for translations, making silent emendations.

5 Cited in Edwards (1996, 10). On Petrarch's Rome and his concept of history, see Christian (2010, 13–15), Greene (1982, 88–93), and Weiss (1969, 30–47).
6 See Hopkins (2017).
7 Őstenberg remarks, "As in all rituals, past and present merged … The city of Rome was also its spectators and … participation, as actor or observer, was a symbol of belonging to the community of Rome, which identified itself by its religious rites and traditions … Rome showed Rome to Rome" (2009, 14). See also Beard (2007) and Brilliant (1999).
8 For additional examples, see Moreno Castillo (2004, 516–17).
9 On Peruzzi's stage design for the comedy *La Calandria* by Cardinal Bernando Dovizi da Bibbiena, see Berzal de Dios (2014) and Hara (2016).
10 In his wandering through the city, Quevedo is solely looking for ancient Rome. The other Rome, the palaces, villas, churches, and chapels that adorn the city's landscape, does not figure in the *silva*. This is the Rome of the papacy, which as Clare Robertson notes, "sought to control building way beyond the confines of the Vatican, with a view to modernizing Rome and enhancing its magnificence." In terms of renovation, the main idea from the beginning was to "transform it from a run-down medieval town to a city that both reflected its imperial past and its importance as the centre of Christendom" (2015, 12).
11 For a study of this sonnet and its sources, see Álvarez Hernández (1989), Cacho Casal (2009, 1174–9), Cuervo (1908), Ferri Coll (1995, 113–20), Lara Garrido (1980), and Skyrme (1982a).
12 For cabinets of curiosities see Findlen (1994, 17–47), Hooper-Greenhill (1992, 78–104), and Bleichmar (2011, 15–30) on the cabinet of the famous Spanish "curioso" Vincencio Juan de Lastanosa, who in Aragón collected books, fine art, and exotica. On Lastanosa, see also Slater (2008).
13 Citations are from Aldrovandi's *Delle statue antiche* (Venice, 1556), which was reprinted in Lucio Mauro, *Le antichità della città di Roma* (Venice, 1557), 181–2 (quoted in Barkan, 1999, 121).
14 On "Roma antigua y moderna," see also Asensio (1983), Cuervo (1908), Rocha de Sigler (1994), and Moreno Castillo's fine assessment of sources (2004).
15 There are three versions of this sonnet, the first from 1613 and the third from 1648, published in González de Salas's *Parnaso*, and the version privileged by Blecua (1969) and Crosby (1967), which I quote here. On this sonnet see, in particular, Durán (1995), Jauralde Pou (1987), and Ferri Coll (2010), with bibliography.
16 On these walls, see Gea Ortigas and Castellanos Oñate (2008).
17 On the poetry of ruins in early modern Spain, see Lara Garrido (1980; 1999, 251–308), Ferri Coll (1995), López Bueno (1990, 77–97), Orozco Díaz ([1947] 1989), Ruiz Sánchez (1999), Skyrme (1982b), and Wardropper (1969). On

ruins in general, see Dillon (2011), Ginsberg (2004), with bibliography, Macaulay (1967), Roth (1997), and " Symposium" (2014). The bibliography is of course extensive. I have noted the studies that have been most useful.

18 On museums, including the dialogic component, see especially Hooper-Greenhill (1992, 2000) and Rutledge (2012).

19 Quevedo wrote two sonnets depicting Philip III's bronze equestrian statue, which may have been modelled after the Capitoline statue of Marcus Aurelius. Exhibited in the Casa de Campo, and standing now in Madrid's Plaza Mayor, Philip's statue was cast by Giambologna (Jean Boulogne) and finished by Pedro Tacca in Florence before it was sent to Spain, sometime after 1614. Two lines of one of the sonnets echo the silva: "Quiere de tu caballo la herradura / pisar líquidas sendas" (1:418; your horse's horseshoes want to tread on liquid paths). This sonnet was a celebration and flattery of the king. As is well known, Quevedo had a troubled relationship with Philip and the Duke of Lerma, and the poem was a way of ingratiating himself to the monarch and perhaps his *valido* as well.

20 The phrase is Armando Petrucci's in his *Writing the Dead* (1998, 43). Quevedo's silva "A los huesos de un rey que se hallaron en un sepulcro" (Blecua 1969, 1:275–7; To the bones of a king which were found in a tomb) rehearses the theme of bodily ruination: "Estas que veis aquí pobres y escuras / ruinas desconocidas [...] estos güesos, sin order derramados, / que en polvo hazañas de la muerte escriben, / ellos fueron un tiempo venerados" (1.275.1–2, 9–11; These lowly and dark unknown ruins that you see [...] these bones, scattered without order, which write feats of death, they once were revered). The tomb, whose inscription was read and unceremoniously trampled by pilgrims, also lies in ruins, its words now silenced.

3. Producing Pastoral Spaces

1 On these and similar works, see in particular Bass (2008b, 173–7) and Bergmann (1979).

2 On space in Lefebvre and de Certeau, see introduction. Lefebvre and de Certeau's notion of space involves textuality as well: "an act of reading is the space produced by the practice of a particular place: a written text, i.e., a place constituted by a system of signs" ([1980] 1988, 117).

3 Quotations from the *Polifemo* are from Alonso ([1967] 1994), stanza followed by line number. Translations are from Dent-Young (2007) and Rivers (1966), with emendations.

4 In a Lacanian reading in *The Madness of Vision*, Christine Buci-Glucksmann, commenting on the luminous bodies of Bernini's *The Ecstasy of Saint Teresa* (1652), ties light to the baroque. After quoting Lacan's thoughts on light (from the perspective of his concept of the gaze), here abbreviated – "That

which is light looks at me, and by means of that light in the depths of my eye, something is painted … something that is an impression, the shimmering of a surface that is not, in advance, situated for me in its distance"– she notes: "'Something is painted': the excessively pleasuring erotic of the baroque evolves into an aesthetic, an *aesthetic of light*" (2015, 40–1; emphasis in original.

5 As Henri Lefebvre would put it, "physical space has no 'reality' without the energy that is deployed within it" ([1974] 1991, 13).

6 Commenting on Salinas's "the poetic insufficiency of reality," Edward Friedman notes that Góngora is "anything but the ultimate nature lover; [he is] the poet who delights in gilding the lily, so to speak, or who gilds the lily merely to make it more beautiful" (2002, 58).

7 For the fruit bag as an ekphrasis of a still life, with attendant notions of abundance, wit, and the ludic, see Castellví Laukamp (2015). On nature and allegory in relation to the fruit bag, see Huergo (2006).

8 On sources, see Vilanova's classic study (1957), Micó (2001), Ponce Cárdenas (2010, 33–45), and Blanco (2012).

9 On the layered image centred on the extravagant exchange of attributes in the interplay between the whiteness of Venus's swan and the luminous eyes on the feathers of Junos's peacock to describe Galatea's beauty, see Alonso ([1967] 1994, 476) and Parker (1977, 24–5, 64–6).

On Galatea as a Venusian figure, see Dolan (1990, 83–8). For an alternate reading, see Torres (2007, 59–63), who argues that though Galatea is a figure of beauty and light, she may be defined more accurately as a "shifting and fluid sign," given the text's uneasy play between appearance and reality. In her recent book (2013), Torres expands on this idea by focusing on Góngora's "self-conscious evocation and elision of meaning" and "freedom from referents" (95–6), a notion very much a part of the present study. For useful assessments of the *Polifemo*, see also Torres (2006).

10 Enrica Cancelliere connects the pearl set in jewellery to baroque art, referencing the *Diccionario de Autoridades* "berrueco" – "cierta especie de perla irregular e imperfecta" (an irregular and imperfect species of pearls) – and Severo Sarduy's neo-baroque (Cancelliere 2006, 61–4).

11 For studies applying Mauss to early modern gift-giving practices, see Davis (2000), Klein (1997), Shephard (2010), and Warwick (1997).

12 Vilanova offers models for Galatea as a statue: Leone's astonishment before Ruggiero's heroic nobility in Ariosto's *Orlando furioso*, "come una statua è immoto" (motionless like a statue), or in Cervantes's *Galatea*, "Atónito quedé y embelesado, / como estátua sin voz de piedra dura" (I was left astonished and enraptured, like a voiceless statue of hard stone) (Vilanova 1957, 2:150).

13 In Ovid's *Metamorphoses*, Juno sets Argus's eyes on the feathers of her peacock (1984, 1:1.722–3), as a tribute to the monster, who was killed by Mercury. The visual pleasure that the lovers have for each other is captured by means of reciprocal images: Acis is identified with the creature whose luminous eyes – the root *arg* means "bright," and Ovid called Argus "stellatus Argus" (star-eyed Argus, 664) – appear on the plumage of Juno's bird, which is identified with Galatea; her eyes shine like stars against the whiteness of her skin.

14 It would seem that in the interactive mirroring of looks, where the lovers are in turn greedy observers and passive objects of contemplation, there is a gendered equal spectatorship. Even though Galatea's predatory gaze in stanza 33 signals mastery, as she is obliquely identified with the eagle ("ave reina"), converting Acis into both object and prey, he is the true predator and she the prey. Details on visual exchange and on melancholia (see below) appeared in a different framing in Barnard (2002).

15 Garcilaso's Third Eclogue serves as precedent, when ivy weaves a canopy, fashioning the shade proper to the *locus amoenus* of the nymphs and their tapestries (Garcilaso de la Vega 1995, lines 57–62).

16 For my discussion of melancholia I have profited from studies by Wittkower and Wittkower (1963) and by Schiesari (1992), in addition to Klibansky, Panofsky, and Saxl (1964). I have also profited from Dolan (1990) on melancholia in Góngora's *Polifemo* and from Soufas (1990) on melancholia in Golden Age texts, including the *Polifemo*.

17 Soufas calls Polyphemus "the mighty poet *faber* whose song-within-song is the only section presented in quotation marks as words directly attributable to their composer" (1990, 136).

18 Friedman interprets the passage as follows: "Polifemo's actions disprove his rhetoric. The professed reformation through love is an illusion. The destructive force cannot be contained, nor can violence be averted" (1995, 70). Anthony Cascardi points out Polyphemus's delusion and considers his song a "pastoral parody" (1980, 133–4).

19 On Polyphemus's monocular vision and theories of optics in relation to Sor Juana's *Primero sueño*, see Bergmann (2013). On the workings of jealousy and looking in the text, see Wagschal (2007), who comments that, unlike the Ovidian version, the story is told in the present and thus Polyphemus's jealousy is more plausible: his violence "explodes before the reader's eyes" (183).

20 Friedman links Cave's notion of *copia* to the *Polifemo*'s rhetoric and ideology and to its multifaceted, all-encompassing abundance (1995, 75).

21 I take my cue from Cave's interpretation of Gargantua's cornucopian codpiece in Rabelais, which stands on the one hand for fertility and plenitude, including its shape, embroidery, and the precious stones

encrusted on the material, and on the other hand for a fall. "Like other Utopian myths," writes Cave, "the cornucopia always presages a fall: its dynamic productivity will sooner or later begin to appear, in the post-lapsarian world, as an emptying out, or as mere flux or repetition" (1979, 183).

4. Staging Myth

An earlier version of this chapter appeared as "Inscribing Transgression, Siting Identity: Arguijo's Phaëton and Ganymede in Painting and Text," in *Writing for the Eyes in the Spanish Golden Age*, edited by Frederick A. de Armas, 109–29 (Lewisburg, PA: Bucknell University Press, 2004).

1 For a study of illustrations of the *Cancionero de Palacio* and the senses, using McGann's concept as a point of departure, see Gerli (2018).

2 On academies, see Brown (1978), Chambers and Quiviger (1995), Cruz (1995), Egido (1990), King (1960, 1963), Pade (2011), Sánchez (1961), Hazañas y la Rúa (1888), and the essays in *The Fairest Flower: The Emergence of Linguistic National Consciousness in Renaissance Europe* (1985), especially Egido, "De las academias a la Academia" (85–94), and Cochrane, "The Renaissance Academics in Their Italian and European Setting" (21–39).

3 On Vasari's house in Arezzo and the ceiling painting, see De Girolami Cheney (2006, 27–43, 91–158) and Berti (1955). For stimulating essays of Vasari's ceiling paintings, letters, and questions of memory, see Baggio, Benigni, and Toccafondi (2015).

4 There are differing interpretations of the iconography of the ceiling paintings. Following Pérez de Moya's *Philosophia secreta*, Brown interprets the paintings as an allegory of the judgment of knowledge and virtue (1978, 77). Welles (1986, 134–5) follows this interpretation. For Angulo Iñiguez, the paintings are in part an allegory of the attainment of glory and a judgment on the quality of poetry (1952, 141–6). Lleó Cañal finds in the ceiling the humanist search for immortality, focusing on Saturn and melancholy, an attribute of Arguijo the poet (1979, 54–5). López Torrijos links the paintings to poetry and fame, as well as to the Iron Age, a period of turmoil and disillusionment in which Justice (Astraea) is absent and Evil rules – a state of affairs in Arguijo's Spain: the attack of Essex on Cádiz in 1596, and the plague that ravished Seville in 1599. López Torrijos also notes the Ovidian subtexts to which Arguijo was drawn (1985, 108), details that she expands in a later study (1999). I thank Jonathan Brown for alerting me to this volume.

5 Vasari explains his psychomachy: "with figures the size of life, is Excellence, who has Envy under her feet and has seized Fortune by the hair, and is beating both the one and the other, and a thing that was much

commented at the time was that as you go round the hall, Fortune being in the middle, from one side Envy seems to be over Fortune and Excellence, and from another side Excellence is over Envy and Fortune, as is seen often happen in real life" (1996, 2:1046). In his ceiling panels there are figures in common with Arguijo's: a painting of the celestial gods and an abduction of Ganymede, but here the boy is riding astride the eagle.

6 On these ceilings, see Fernández López (1999, 159–71), Lleó Cañal (1999, 173–81), Brown (1978, 77–80), and Valdivieso and Serrera (1979).

7 Vranich in his edition of Arguijo's works (1985, 123–4) gives as examples Fernando de Herrera and the Count of Villamediana. Herrera writes of Phaëthon: "Grande fue, aunque infelice, tu osadía / ¡o valeroso hijo de Climene!" (1992, sonnet 108, 255; Your daring was great, though unhappy, oh courageous son of Clymene!) Villamediana in his "Fábula de Faetón" alludes to a "culpa gloriosamente peregrina" (glorious fault, seldom seen) and calls Phaëthon "hijo [...] digno del autor del día / [...] que pudo acreditar con su osadía, / si no feliz, famoso atrevimiento, [...] / [y] que su fama adquirió con su rüina" (1969, 205–6; a son ... worthy of the maker of days ... who could validate with his daring a famous, if unhappy, undertaking ... [and] who acquired fame through his ruin).

8 Arguijo may have been familiar with Michelangelo's *Ganymede* through Pacheco's copy, which had belonged to Arias Montano, as mentioned earlier. Frederick de Armas suggests that Michelangelo's *Ganymede* and another drawing that had been sent to Cavalieri, *The Fall of Phaëthon*, may have inspired Arguijo's coupling of the two figures in his ceiling paintings (2000, 250), an interpretation strengthened by the fact that in the upper centre section of Michelangelo's *Phaëthon* appears a small picture of Ganymede riding the eagle. In addition to his homoerotic reading of Arguijo's Ganymede, de Armas presents an astrological reading (247–52).

9 On the *Ganymede* drawing, see Branna Perlman (2000, 115–16) and Saslow (1986, 17–62).

10 Michelangelo often writes of love as both sexual delight and celestial bliss, making the Neoplatonic interpretations of his *Ganymede* all the more plausible. As Barkan points out, his sonnets echo the *Ganymede* drawing in its reference to feathers, wings, and upward flight (1991, 82).

11 The pertinent lines from Fracastoro read:

Ne timeas, Troiane Puer, quod in ardua tantum
Tolleris a terra: quod rostro, atque unguibus uncis
Te complexa ferox volucris per inania portat.
Audistine unquam sublimis nomen Olympi?
Audistine Jovis tonitru, qui fulmina torquet,
Qui pluit in terras, cui templa arasque dicatis

Vos homines, taurosque tua mactatis in Ida
Quique etiam vestri est, si nescis, sanguinis auctor?
Ille ego sum. Non te haec volucris, sed Juppiter est, qui
Haud praeda captus, cari sed amore Nepotis
In summum amplexu innocuo te portat Olympum:
Astra ubi tot spectare soles, ubi pulcher obit Sol
Ortusque occasusque suos, ubi candida noctes
Currit Luna notens, Auroram Lucifer anteit.
Hic ego te in numero superum, domibusque deorum. (1954, 52–3)

(Do not fear, Trojan boy, that you are taken so high from earth, that the fierce bird carries you embraced with his beak and hooked claws through the emptiness. Have you not heard of the sublime name of Olympus? Have you not heard of Jove, who hurls thunderbolts, who unleashes rain on earth, to whom men have dedicated temples and altars and sacrificed bulls in Ida? And who among you does not know the bloody author? I am he. It is not that bird but Jupiter who carries you, not as a captured prey but as a beloved boy in innocent embrace, to the high Olympus, where you will watch the stars, where the beautiful Sun sets in the west, where the shining Moon chases the white night [and] Lucifer precedes the Dawn. I bring you here to the upper world and the houses of the gods.)

Stanko Vranich, in his edition with commentary (Arguijo 1985), offers details of Arguijo's adaptation of Fracastoro (158–62).

12 In the early modern period there are also playful readings of the myth of Ganymede. Panofsky cites a letter of 7 July 1533 from Sebastiano del Piombo to Michelangelo: "As to the painting in the vault of the lantern [in a fresco of the Medici Chapel] our Lord [Pope Clement VII] leaves it to you to do what you like. I think the Ganymede would look nice there, you could give him a halo so that he would appear as St. John of the Apocalypse carried to Heaven" (1967, 212–13). Panofsky notes that, given Sebastiano's mocking style in his letters, this must be understood as a joke, although he has as his model the tradition of Christian allegoresis that survives well into the Renaissance.

5. A Mystic and Her Objects

An earlier version of this chapter appeared as "Aristocrat and Mystic: Writing the Material in Luisa de Carvajal y Mendoza," in *Perspectives on Early Modern Women in Iberia and the Americas: Studies in Law, Society, Art, and Literature in Honor of Anne J. Cruz*, ed. Adrienne L. Martín and María Cristina Quintero (New York: Escribana Books, 2015), 459–79.

1 Carvajal also had done needlework ("labores") to support herself and her companion in her impoverished life in Madrid, as she mentions in her Vow of Poverty (Rhodes 2000, 108). When it came to earning a living, as Rhodes comments, she did not share the strict rules of poverty prescribed by Teresa of Ávila, whose words of caution about nuns' work excluded luxury threads: "Their earnings must not come from work requiring careful attention to fine details but from spinning and sewing or other unrefined labor that does not occupy the mind as to keep it from the Lord. Nor should they do work with gold or silver" (*Constitutions* 9; cited in Rhodes 2000, 281n26). On Carvajal's manual labour, see Redworth (2008, 44). On her letters in networking and self-fashioning, see Pando-Canteli (2016).

2 Abad (1966a, 141). All references to Carvajal's autobiography come from this edition.

3 For details on Carvajal's life, I have drawn on Abad (1966b) and his introduction to his edition of *Escritos autobiográficos* (Abad 1966a, 9–124). I have also drawn from Cruz (2014, 1–35).

4 On Carvajal's emphasis on eroticism and the body in her sonnets, see Fox (2008). Cruz mentions how, in her autobiography, Carvajal dwells on her uncle's "good looks" (1992, 99–100), as she focuses on Christ's own. Her uncle cuts a dashing figure: "No muy alto ni pequeño; blanquísimo, y el cabello como un mismo oro, algo asortijado. Sus ojos eran realísimos y demonstradores de su ánimo" (Abad 1966a, 150; Neither tall nor short, extremely fair, and his hair was like gold, somewhat curly. His eyes were truly alive and mirrors of his spirit). He was for her a poet and a singer, wise and "docto," whose words had counselled her in religious matters and in questions of conduct. He was, at least in her memory, a holy figure: "yo le miraba siempre con notable respeto y reverencia, como si estuviere delante un cuerpo sancto [*sic*]" (156; I looked upon him with much respect and reverence as if I had before me a holy presence).

5 On the festishized body, see Vickers (1982) and Kritzman (1991). On Petrarch and the beauty of Christ's body parts in relation to the Passion in Carvajal's poem, see Cruz (2009, 260–3).

6 Quotations from Carvajal's poetry are from Abad (1965), with poem number followed by line number and page number.

7 On the use of images and vision in autobiographies written by nuns in Counter-Reformation Spain, see Alcalá Galán (2015, 281–399). For a novel interpretation of religious art through a multisensory approach, see Johnson (2020, 1179–1234).

8 Carvajal's keen interest in relics is revealed in England, where she collected body parts of Catholics who had been executed and quartered. In her letter to the Marquis of Caracena, 16 April 1611, she writes about how the bodies of a priest and a monk were brought to her house: "Para aderezarlos,

pusieron en el suelo el un brazo con su medio pecho y espalda, y el otro con el otro medio. Extraño espectáculo y motivo de oración, ver aquellas armas tan frágiles con que pelearon tan sin fragilidad, animosamente. [...] He hecho que me dé algunos pedazos el padre cuyos suyos son; pero no pude sacarle lo que quisiera de las santas reliquias" (Abad 1965, 324–5). (In order to prepare them, they put one of the arms with its half of the back and chest on the floor and then did the same with the other one. What an extraordinary spectacle and inspiration to prayer it was to see such frail weapons with which they fought, yet without any frailty at all and with such spirit ... I managed to get some pieces from the father to whom they belong, although I could not get as much as I wanted of the holy relics from him; Redworth 2012, 2:157).

9 Cruz reminds us that the body of Christ is an integral part of the poetry of meditation and links it to Ignatius's *Spiritual Exercises* (1992, 107). Cruz's studies on Carvajal's poetry (1994, 1995, 1999, 2004) and Cruz's edition on her life and writings (2014), with bibliography, have been most helpful in this study. See also Rhodes (1998) and Bradburn-Ruster (2000).

10 Carvajal confesses her devotion to her meditation on the seven "derramamientos de sangre" (the shedding of blood), which she lists: "la circuncisión, sudor en el güerto (huerto), azotes a la columna, coronación de espinas, el desnudarle la vestidura, enclavar en la cruz y la lanzada" (Abad 1966a, 152; the circumcision, bloody sweat in the garden, lashing at the column, the crowning with thorns, the disrobing of his clothing, the nailing to the cross, and the lance wound).

11 Bouza (1999, 272) notes that there were several volumes by Luis de Granada in the library, including the *Doctrina espiritual, Guía de pecadores,* and *Libro de la oración y meditación* (numbers 116 and 232–3 in the inventory).

12 García-Nieto Onrubia mentions that "pebetes," "cazoletas," and "pastillas" were used as "perfumadores ambientales" and points to Fray Luis de León's *La perfecta casada* as a possible source: "el gasto de las mujeres es todo en el aire [...] en volantes, en guantes, en pebetes, y cazoletas" (Carvajal y Mendoza 1990, 77nn43–4; emphasis in the original).

13 On class, status, and codes of honour in early modern Spain, see Maravall (1979) and Domínguez Ortiz (1973).

Epilogue

1 My book is part of a growing field in visual and material culture in early modern Spanish literature. There are studies on diverse topics: the role of portraits in drama by Laura Bass (2008a), on clothing and ornaments in autobiographical writings by Encarnación Juárez Almendros (2006), on art

inscriptions by Emilie Bergmann (1979), on optics by Enrique García Santo-Tomás (2009a, 2017). Frederick de Armas (2006) examines how Cervantes was inspired by Italian frescoes, paintings, and sculptures, and Ana Laguna (2009) studies Cervantes's texts in relation to Italian, Spanish, and Flemish art. Essays in collections edited by García Santo-Tomás (2009b), de Armas (2004), Barnard and de Armas (2013), and a recent special issue of *Calíope: Journal of the Society for Renaissance and Baroque Hispanic Poetry*, edited by Albert Lloret and Miguel Martínez (2018), cover a wide range of topics in this expanding field of inquiry.

Works Cited

Abad, Camilo María (SJ), ed. 1965. *Doña Luisa de Carvajal y Mendoza (1566–1614): Epistolario y poesías*. Biblioteca de Autores Españoles, 179. Madrid: Atlas.

– ed. 1966a. *Escritos autobiográficos*. Barcelona: Juan Flors.

– 1966b. *Una misionera española en la Inglaterra del siglo XVII:Doña Luisa de Carvajal y Mendoza (1566–1614)*. Comillas: Universidad Pontificia.

Agamben, Giorgio. 1993. *Stanzas: Word and Phantasm in Western Culture*. Translated by Ronald L. Martinez. Minneapolis: University of Minnesota Press.

Alberti, Leon Battista. 1966. *De pictura*. Translated by John R. Spencer. New Haven, CT: Yale University Press.

Alcalá Galán, Mercedes. 2015. "'Así como lo pintan por acá': Iconografía contrarreformista en las Vidas de monjas." In *Perspectives on Early Modern Women in Iberia and the Americas: Studies in Law, Society, Art, and Literature in Honor of Anne J. Cruz*, edited by Adrienne L. Martín and María Cristina Quintero, 381–99. New York: Escribana Books.

Allen, Paul C. 2000. *Philip III and the Pax Hispanica, 1598–1621: The Failure of Grand Strategy*. New Haven, CT: Yale University Press.

Alonso, Dámaso, ed. (1967) 1994. *Góngora y el "Polifemo."* Madrid: Gredos.

Álvarez Hernández, Arturo R. 1989. "Fuentes y originalidad en un soneto de Quevedo consagrado a Roma, sepultada en sí misma." *Canente* 6: 13–27. doi:10.1086/650026.

Angulo Íñiguez, Diego. 1952. *La mitología y el arte español del Renacimiento*. Madrid: Maestre.

Appadurai, Arjun, ed. 1986. *The Social Life of Things: Commodities in Cultural Perspective*. Cambridge: Cambridge University Press.

Arguijo, Juan de. 1971. *Obra poética*. Edited by Stanko B. Vranich. Madrid: Castalia.

Asensio, Eugenio. 1983. "Un Quevedo incógnito: Las *silvas*." *Edad de Oro*, no. 2: 13–48. https://dialnet.unirioja.es.

Augustine, Saint. 1998. *The City of God against the Pagans*. Edited and translated by R.W. Dyson. Cambridge: Cambridge University Press.

Baer, Ronni. 2008. "El Greco to Velázquez: Artists of the Reign of Philip III." In *El Greco to Velázquez: Art during the Reign of Philip III*, edited by Sarah Schroth and Ronni Baer, 41–75. Boston: Museum of Fine Arts.

Baggio, Silvia, Paola Benigni, and Diana Toccafondi, eds. 2015. *Giorgio Vasari: La Casa, le Carte, il Teatro della Memoria*. Florence: Olschki.

Bakhtin, Mikhail. 1989. *The Dialogic Imagination: Four Essays*. Edited by Michael Holquist and translated by Caryl Emerson and Michael Holquist. Austin: University of Texas Press.

Bal, Mieke. 2001. *Looking In: The Art of Viewing*. Introduction by Norman Bryson. London: Routledge.

Barkan, Leonard. 1991. *Transuming Passion: Ganymede and the Erotics of Humanism*. Stanford, CA: Stanford University Press.

– 1999. *Unearthing the Past: Archaeology and Aesthetics in the Making of Renaissance Culture*. New Haven, CT: Yale University Press.

Barnard, Mary E. 2002. "The Gaze and the Mirror: Vision, Desire, and Identity in Góngora's *Fábula de Polifemo y Galatea*." *Calíope: Journal of the Society for Renaissance and Baroque Hispanic Poetry* 8, no 1: 69–85.

– 2014. *Garcilaso de la Vega and the Material Culture of Renaissance Europe*. Toronto: University of Toronto Press.

Barnard, Mary E., and Frederick A. de Armas, eds. 2013. *Objects of Culture in the Literature of Imperial Spain*. Toronto: University of Toronto Press.

Barthes, Roland. 1979. "From Work to Text." In *Textual Strategies: Perspectives in Post-Structuralist Criticism*, edited by Josué Harari, 73–81. Ithaca, NY: Cornell University Press.

Bass, Laura R. 2008a. *The Drama of the Portrait: Theater and Visual Culture in Early Modern Spain*. University Park: Pennsylvania State University Press.

– 2008b. "The Treasury of the Language: Literary Invention in Philip III's Spain." In *El Greco to Velázquez: Art during the Reign of Philip III*, edited by Sarah Schroth and Ronni Baer, 147–81. Boston: Museum of Fine Arts.

– 2017. "The Poet in Painting: Góngora's Portraits and the Politics of the Paragone." In *Velázquez Re-Examined: Theory, History, Poetry, and Theatre*, edited by Giles Knox and Tanya J. Tiffany, 21–44. Turnhout, Belgium: Brepols.

Beard, Mary. 2007. *The Roman Triumph*. Cambridge, MA: Belknap Press of Harvard University Press.

Bell, Stephen M. 1984. "The Book of Life and Death: Quevedo and the Printing Press." *Hispanic Journal* 5, no. 2: 7–15. https://www.jstor.org.

Benzi, Fabio, ed. 2000. *Sisto IV: Le Arti a Roma nel Primo Rinascimento*. Atti del Convegno Internazionale di Studi. Rome: Edizioni dell'Associazione Culturale Shakespeare and Company 2.

Bergmann, Emilie L. 1979. *Art Inscribed: Essays on Ekphrasis in Spanish Golden Age Poetry*. Harvard Studies in Romance Languages, 35. Cambridge, MA: Harvard University Press.

– 2013. "Sor Juana, Góngora and Ideologies of Perception." *Caliope: Journal of the Society for Renaissance and Baroque Hispanic Poetry* 18, no. 2: 116–38. https://muse.jhu.edu.

Berti, L. 1955. *La casa del Vasari in Arezzo e il suo Museo*. Catalogo. Florence and Arezzo: Salimbeni.

Berzal de Dios, Javier. 2014. "Conjuring the Concept of Rome: Alterity and Synecdoche in Peruzzi's Design for *La Calandria*." *Sixteenth Century Journal* 45, no. 1: 25–50. https://www.jstor.org.

Beverley, John R. 1980. *Aspects of Góngora's Soledades*. Purdue University Monographs in Romance Languages. Amsterdam: John Benjamins.

Blanco, Mercedes. 2012. "Del *Polifemo* griego al barroco: Un mito y sus imágenes." *Ínsula* 67, nos. 781–2: 3–6. https://dialnet.unirioja.es.

Blecua, José Manuel. 1969. *Francisco de Quevedo: Obra poética*. Vol 1. Madrid: Castalia.

– ed. 1983. *Lope de Vega: Obras poéticas*. Barcelona: Planeta.

Bleichmar, Daniela. 2011. "Seeing the World in a Room: Looking at Exotica in Early Modern Collections." In *Collecting across Cultures: Material Exchanges in the Early Modern Atlantic World*, edited by Daniela Bleichmar and Peter C. Mancall, 15–30. Philadelphia: University of Pennsylvania Press.

Bouza, Fernando. 1999. "Docto y devoto: La biblioteca del Marqués de Almazán y Conde de Monteagudo (Madrid, 1591)." In *Hispania-Austria II: Die Epoche Phillips II (1556–1598) / La época de Felipe II (1556–1598)*, edited by Friedrich Edelmeyer, 247–310. Vienna: Verlag für Geschichte und Politik; Munich: Oldenbourg.

Bowie, Malcolm. 1991. *Lacan*. Cambridge, MA: Harvard University Press.

Boym, Svetlana. 2010. "Ruinophilia: Appreciation of Ruins." In *Atlas of Transformation*, edited by Zbynek Baladrán and Vit Havránek, 555–7. Prague: Tranzit.

Bradburn-Ruster, Michael. 2000. "The Beautiful Dove, the Body Divine: Luisa de Carvajal y Mendoza's Mystical Poetics." In *The Mystical Gesture: Essays on Medieval and Early Modern Spiritual Culture in Honor of Mary E. Giles*, edited by Robert Boenig, 159–68. Aldershot, UK: Ashgate.

Branna Perlman, Julia. 2000. "Looking at Venus and Ganymede Anew: Problems and Paradoxes in the Relations among Neoplatonic Writing and Renaissance Art." In *Antiquity and Its Interpreters*, edited by Alina Payne, Ann Kuttner, and Rebekah Smick, 110–25. Cambridge: Cambridge University Press.

Bresson, Robert. 2016. *Notes on the Cinematograph*. Translated by Jonathan Griffin. New York: New York Review Books.

Brilliant, Richard. 1999. "'Let the Trumpets Roar!' The Roman Triumph." *Studies in the History of Art* 56: 220–9.

Brown, Jonathan. 1978. *Images and Ideas in Seventeenth-Century Painting*. Princeton, NJ: Princeton University Press.

Buci-Glucksmann, Christine. 2015. *The Madness of Vision: On Baroque Aesthetics*. Translated by Dorothy Z. Baker. Athens: Ohio University Press.

Bynum, Caroline Walker. 1982. *Jesus as Mother: Studies in the Spirituality of the High Middle Ages*. Berkeley: University of California Press.

– 2011. *Christian Materiality: An Essay on Religion in Late Medieval Europe*. New York: Zone Books.

Byrne, Susan. 2015. *Ficino in Spain*. Toronto: University of Toronto Press.

Cacho Casal, Rodrigo. 2009. "The Memory of Ruins: Quevedo's Silva to 'Roma antigua y moderna.'" *Renaissance Quarterly* 62, no. 4: 1167–203.

– 2012a. "El pincel y el alfabeto de las imágenes." In *La esfera del ingenio: Las silvas de Quevedo y la tradición europea*, 89–127. Madrid: Biblioteca Nueva.

– 2012b. "Quevedo y la filología de autor: Edición de la silva *El pincel*." *Criticón*, no. 114: 179–212. doi:10.4000/criticon.1442.

Cancelliere, Enrica. 2006. *Góngora: Itinerarios de la visión*. Translated by Rafael Bonilla and Linda Garosi. Córdoba: Diputación de Córdoba.

Candelas Colodrón, Manuel Ángel. 1995. "Las silvas de Quevedo." In *Estudios sobre Quevedo: Quevedo desde Santiago entre dos aniversarios*, edited by Santiago Fernández Mosquera, 161–85. Santiago de Compostela: Universidad de Santiago de Compostela.

– 1996. "La silva 'El pincel' de Quevedo: La teoría pictórica y la alabanza de pintores al servicio del dogma contrarreformista." *Bulletin Hispanique* 98, no. 1: 85–95. https://www.persee.fr.

– 1997. *Las silvas de Quevedo*. Vigo: Universidade de Vigo.

Carducho, Vicente. 1979. *Diálogos de la pintura*. Edited by Francisco Calvo Serraller. Madrid: Turner.

Carreira, Antonio. 1997. "Quevedo y su elogio de la lectura." *La Perinola*, no. 1: 87–97. https://hdl.handle.net/10171/4547.

Carroll, Maureen. 2006. *Spirits of the Dead: Roman Funerary Commemoration in Western Europe*. Oxford: Oxford University Press.

Carvajal y Mendoza, Luisa de. 1990. *Poesías completas*. Edited by María Luisa García-Nieto Onrubia. Badajoz, Spain: Diputación Provincial de Badajoz.

Cascardi, Anthony. 1980. "The Exit from Arcadia: Reevaluation of the Pastoral in Virgil, Garcilaso, and Góngora." *Journal of Hispanic Philology* 4: 119–41. https://pureadmin.qub.ac.uk.

Castellví Laukamp, Luis. 2015. "Food for Thought: The Fruit Still Life in Góngora's *Polifemo*." *Bulletin of Hispanic Studies* 92, no. 6: 629–44. doi:10.3828/bhs.2015.38.

Cave, Terence. 1979. *The Cornucopian Text: Problems of Writing in the French Renaissance*. Oxford: Oxford University Press.

Certeau, Michel de. (1980) 1988. *The Practice of Everyday Life*. Translated by Steven F. Randall. Berkeley: University of California Press.

– 1988. *The Writing of History*. Translated by Tom Conley. New York: Columbia University Press.

Chambers, D.S., and F. Quiviger, eds. 1995. *Italian Academies of the Sixteenth Century*. London. Warburg Institute, University of London.

Chartier, Roger. 2007. *Inscription and Erasure: Literature and Written Culture from the Eleventh to the Eighteenth Century*. Translated by Arthur Goldhammer. Philadelphia: University of Pennsylvania Press.

Christian, Kathleen Wren. 2010. *Empire without End: Antiquities Collections in Renaissance Rome, c. 1350–1527*. New Haven, CT: Yale University Press.

Cochrane, Eric W. 1985. "The Renaissance Academies in Their Italian and European Setting." In *The Fairest Flower: The Emergence of Linguistic National Consciousness in Renaissance Europe*, International Conference of the Center for Medieval and Renaissance Studies, University of California, Los Angeles, 12–13 December 1983, 21–39. Florence: L'Accademia.

Coffin, David R. 1979. *The Villa in the Life of Renaissance Rome*. Princeton, NJ: Princeton University Press.

Collins, Marsha S. 2002. *The "Soledades," Góngora's Masque of the Imagination*. Columbia: University of Missouri Press.

Colomer, José Luis. 2002. "Uso y función de la miniatura en la corte de Felipe IV: Velázquez miniaturista." *Boletín del Museo del Prado* 20, no. 38: 65–83. http://www.openbibart.fr.

Columbus, Christopher. 1982. *Cristóbal Colón: Textos y documentos completos. Relaciones de viajes, cartas, y memoriales*. Edited by Consuelo Varela. Madrid: Alianza.

Cosgrove, Denis. 1993. *The Palladian Landscape: Geographical Change and Its Cultural Representations in Sixteenth-Century Italy*. University Park: Pennsylvania State University Press.

Covarrubias Orozco, Sebastián de. 1984. *Tesoro de la lengua castellana o española*. Madrid: Turner.

Crosby, James O. 1955. "Quevedo's Alleged Participation in the Conspiracy of Venice." *Hispanic Review* 23, no. 4: 259–73. https://www.jstor.org.

– 1966. "Quevedo, the Greek Anthology, and Horace. *Romance Philology* 19, no. 3: 435–49. https://www.jstor.org.

– 1967. *En torno a la poesía de Quevedo*. Madrid: Castalia.

– ed. 1994. *Francisco de Quevedo: Poesía varia*. Madrid: Cátedra.

Cruz, Anne J. 1992. "Chains of Desire: Luisa de Carvajal y Mendoza's Poetics of Penance." In *Estudios sobre escritoras hispanas en Madrid: En honor de*

Georgina Sabat-Rivers, edited by Lou Charnon Deutsch, 97–112. Madrid: Castalia.

– 1994. "Luisa de Carvajal y Mendoza y su conexión jesuita." In *La mujer y su representación en las literaturas hispánicas*, edited by Juan Villegas, 97–104. Irvine, CA: Asociación Internacional de Hispanistas.

– 1995. "Art of the State: The *Academias Literarias* as Sites of Symbolic Economies in Golden Age Spain." *Calíope: Journal of the Society for Renaissance and Baroque Hispanic Poetry* 1, no. 1–2: 72–95. https://muse.jhu.edu.

– 1999. *Discourses of Poverty: Social Reform and the Picaresque Novel in Early Modern Spain*. Toronto: University of Toronto Press.

– 2009. "Words Made Flesh: Luisa de Carvajal's Eucharistic Poetry." In *"En desagravio de las damas": Studies of Women's Poetry of the Golden Age*, edited by Julián Olivares, 255–69. London: Tamesis.

– ed. and trans. 2014. *The Life and Writings of Luisa de Carvajal y Mendoza*. Toronto: Centre for Reformation and Renaissance Studies.

Cuervo, Rufino José. 1908. "Dos poesías de Quevedo a Roma." *Revue Hispanique* 18: 432–8. https://www.uniliber.com.

Culler, Jonathan. 1981. "Apostrophe." In *The Pursuit of Signs: Semiotics, Literature, Deconstruction*, 135–54. Ithaca, NY: Cornell University Press.

Curran, Brian A. 2007. *The Egyptian Renaissance: The Afterlife of Ancient Egypt in Early Modern Italy*. Chicago: University of Chicago Press.

Curran, Brian A., Anthony Grafton, Pamela O. Long, and Benjamin Weiss. 2009. *Obelisk: A History*. Cambridge, MA: Burndy Library, MIT Press.

Curtius, Ernst Robert. 1963. *European Literature and the Latin Middle Ages*. Translated by Willard R. Trask. New York: Harper & Row.

Davis, Natalie Zemon. 2000. *The Gift in Sixteenth-Century France*. Madison: University of Wisconsin Press.

de Armas, Frederick A. 1996. "The Allure of the Oriental Other: Titian's Rossa Sultana and Lope de Vega's *La santa liga*." In *Brave New Words: Studies in Spanish Golden Age Literature*, edited by Edward H. Friedman and Catherine Larson, 191–208. New Orleans, LA: University Press of the South.

– 2000. "Deflecting Desire: The Portrayal of Ganymede in Arguijo's Art and Poetry." In *Lesbianism and Homosexuality in Early Modern Spain: Literature and Theater in Context*, edited by María José Delgado and Alain Saint-Saëns, 235–56. New Orleans, LA: University Press of the South.

– ed. 2004. *Writing for the Eyes in the Spanish Golden Age*. Lewisburg, PA: Bucknell University Press.

– 2006. *Quixotic Frescoes: Cervantes and Italian Renaissance Art*. Toronto: University of Toronto Press.

– 2019. "Cervantes' Hermetic Architectures: The Dangers Outside in *Persiles* IV." In *Cervantes' Persiles and the Travails of Romance*, edited by Marina Brownlee, 17–34. Toronto: University of Toronto Press.

De Girolami Cheney, Liana. 2006. *The Homes of Giorgio Vasari*. New York and Oxford: Peter Lang.

De Grazia, Margreta, Maureen Quilligan, and Peter Stallybrass, eds. 1996. *Subject and Object in Renaissance Culture*. Cambridge: Cambridge University Press.

de Man, Paul. 1984. *The Rhetoric of Romanticism*. New York: Columbia University Press.

Dent-Young, John, ed. and trans. 2007. *Selected Poems of Luis de Góngora: A Bilingual Edition*. Chicago and London: University of Chicago Press.

Diccionario de Autoridades. 1984. Edición facsímil. Madrid: Gredos.

Dillon, Brian, ed. 2011. *Ruins*. Cambridge, MA: MIT Press.

Dolan, Kathleen Hunt. 1990. *Cyclopean Song: Melancholy and Aestheticism in Góngora's "Fábula de Polifemo y Galatea."* North Carolina Studies in the Romance Languages and Literatures, 236. Chapel Hill: University of North Carolina Press.

Domínguez Ortiz, Antonio. 1973. *Las clases privilegiadas en la España del Antiguo Régimen*. Madrid: Istmo.

Dupont, Florence. 1992. *Daily Life in Ancient Rome*. Translated by Christopher Woodall. Oxford: Oxford University Press.

Durán, Manuel. 1995. "Existential Baroque: Francisco de Quevedo's Sonnet 'Miré los muros de la patria mía.'" *Caliope: Journal of the Society for Renaissance and Baroque Hispanic Poetry* 1, nos. 1–2: 169–85. https://www.muse.jhu.edu.

Edwards, Catharine. 1996. *Writing Rome: Textual Approaches to the City*. Cambridge: Cambridge University Press.

– 2015. "Absent Presence in Seneca's *Epistles:* Philosophy and Friendship." In *The Cambridge Companion to Seneca*, edited by Shadi Bartsch and Alessandro Schiesaro, 41–53. Cambridge: Cambridge University Press.

Egido, Aurora. 1985. "De las academias a la Academia." In *The Fairest Flower: The Emergence of Linguistic National Consciousness in Renaissance Europe* (1985), International Conference of the Center for Medieval and Renaissance Studies, University of California, Los Angeles, 12–13 December 1983, 85–94. Florence: L'Accademia.

– 1990. "Literatura efímera: Oralidad y escritura en los certámenes y academias." In *Fronteras de la poesía en el barroco*, 138–163. Barcelona: Crítica.

Elliott, J.H. (1963) 2002. *Imperial Spain, 1469–1716*. New York: Penguin.

Elsner, Jaś. 2007. *Roman Eyes: Visuality and Subjectivity in Art and Text*. Princeton, NJ: Princeton University Press.

– 2015. "Relic, Icon, and Architecture: The Material Articulation of the Holy in East Christian Art." In *Saints and Sacred Matter: The Cult of Relics in Byzantium and Beyond*, edited by Cynthia Hahn and Holger A. Klein, 13–40. Washington, DC: Dumbarton Oaks Research Library and Collection.

The Fairest Flower: The Emergence of Linguistic National Consciousness in Renaissance Europe. International Conference of the Center for Medieval and Renaissance Studies, University of California, Los Angeles, 12–13 December 1983. Florence: L'Accademia.

Fernández López, José. 1999. "Los techos pintados del Palacio Arzobispal de Sevilla." In *Velázquez y Sevilla: Estudios y Catálogo.* 2: 159–71. Seville: Junta de Andalucía. https://dialnet.unirioja.es.

Feros, Antonio. 2000. *Kingship and Favoritism in the Spain of Philip III, 1598–1621.* Cambridge: Cambridge University Press.

– 2002. *El duque de Lerma: Realeza y privanza en la España de Felipe III.* Madrid: Marcial Pons.

– 2008. "Art and Spanish Society: The Historical Context, 1577–1623." In *El Greco to Velázquez: Art during the Reign of Philip III,* edited by Sarah Schroth and Ronni Baer, 15–39. Boston: Museum of Fine Arts.

Ferri Coll, José María. 1995. *Las ciudades cantadas: El tema de las ruinas en la poesía española del Siglo de Oro.* Alicante: Universidad de Alicante.

– 2010. "Miré los muros de la patria mía y la tradición poética de las ruinas." *Bulletin of Hispanic Studies* 87, no. 5: 523–43. doi:10.3828/bhs.2010.16.

Findlen, Paula. 1994. *Possessing Nature: Museums, Collecting, and Scientific Culture in Early Modern Italy.* Berkeley: University of California Press.

Foucault, Michel. 1986. "Of Other Spaces." *Diacritics* 16, no. 1: 22–7. doi:10.1163/9789042026032_014.

Fox, Gwyn. 2008. "Luisa de Carvajal: More Martha than Mary." In *Subtle Subversions: Reading Golden Age Sonnets by Iberian Women,* 246–83. Washington, DC: Catholic University of America Press.

Fracastoro, Girolamo. 1954. *Carmina.* Edited by Giovanni Pellegrini. Verona: Edizioni di Vita Veronese.

Freud, Sigmund. (1961) 2005. *Civilization and Its Discontents.* Edited and translated by James Strachey. New York: Norton.

– 1978. "Mourning and Melancholia." In *The Standard Edition of the Complete Psychological Works of Sigmund Freud,* translated by James Strachey, 14:243–58. London: Hogarth.

Friedman, Edward H. 1995. "Creative Space: Ideologies of Discourse in Góngora's *Polifemo.*" In *Cultural Authority in Golden Age Spain,* edited by Marina S. Brownlee and Hans Ulrich Gumbrecht, 51–78. Baltimore, MD: Johns Hopkins University Press.

– 2002. "Realities and Poets: Góngora, Cervantes, and the Nature of Art." *Caliope: Journal of the Society for Renaissance and Baroque Hispanic Poetry* 8, no. 1: 55–68. https://www.muse.jhu.edu.

Gallego, Julián. *Visión y símbolos en la pintura española del Siglo de Oro.* Madrid: Cátedra, 1984.

García Santo-Tomás, Enrique. 2009a. "Fortunes of the Occhiali Politici in Early Modern Spain: Optics, Vision, Points of View." *PMLA* 124, no.1: 59–75.

– 2009b. *Materia crítica: formas de ocio y de consumo en la cultura áurea*. Madrid and Frankfurt: Iberoamericana/Vervuert.

– 2017. *The Refracted Muse: Literature and Optics in Early Modern Spain*. Translated by Vincent Barletta. Chicago: University of Chicago Press.

Garcilaso de la Vega. 1995. *Garcilaso de la Vega: Obra poética y textos en prosa*. Edited by Bienvenido Morros. Barcelona: Crítica.

Garoian, Charles R. 2001. "Performing the Museum." *Studies in Art Education* 42, no. 3: 234–48. doi:10.1080/00393541.2001.11651700.

Gea Ortigas, Isabel, and José Manuel Castellanos Oñate. 2008. *Madrid musulmán, judío y cristiano: Las murallas medievales de Madrid*. Madrid: Ediciones La Librería.

Gerli, E. Michael. 2018. "Sight, Sound, Scent, and Sense: Reading the *Cancionero de Palacio*." In *Beyond Sight: Engaging the Senses in Iberian Literatures and Cultures, 1200–1750*, edited by Ryan D. Giles and Steven Wagschal, 125–40. Toronto: University of Toronto Press.

Ginsberg, Robert. 2004. *The Aesthetics of Ruins*. Amsterdam: Rodopi.

Gowing, Alain M. 2005. *Empire and Memory: The Representation of the Roman Republic in Imperial Culture*. Cambridge: Cambridge University Press.

Grafton, Anthony. 2002. *Leon Battista Alberti: Master Builder of the Italian Renaissance*. Cambridge, MA: Harvard University Press.

The Greek Anthology. 1970. Edited and translated by W.R. Paton. 5 vols. Cambridge, MA: Harvard University Press.

Greenblatt, Stephen. 1991. "Resonance and Wonder." In *Exhibiting Cultures: The Poetics and Politics of Museum Display*, edited by Ivan Karp and Steven D. Lavine, 42–56. Washington, DC, and London: Smithsonian Institution Press.

Greene, Thomas. 1982. *The Light in Troy: Imitation and Discovery in Renaissance Poetry*. New Haven, CT: Yale University Press.

Gutiérrez, Carlos M. 2005. *La espada, el rayo y la pluma*. West Lafayette, IN: Purdue University Press.

Hagstrum, Jean H. (1958) 1987. *The Sister Arts: The Tradition of Literary Pictorialism and English Poetry from Dryden to Gray*. Chicago: University of Chicago Press.

Hara, Mari Yoko. 2016. "Capturing Eyes and Moving Souls: Peruzzi's Perspective Set for *La Calandria* and the Performative Agency of Architectural Bodies." *Renaissance Studies* 31, no. 4: 586–607. doi:10.1111/rest.12249.

Hazañas y la Rúa, Joaquín. 1888. *Noticia de las academias literarias, artísticas y científicas de los siglos XVII y* XVIII. Seville: Torres.

Heath, Stephen. 1981. *Questions of Cinema*. Bloomington: Indiana University Press.

Heisenberg, Werner. 1972. *Physics and Beyond: Encounters and Conversations*. Translated by Arnold J. Pomerans. New York: Harper & Row.

Herrera, Fernando de. 1992. *Poesías*. Edited by Victoriano Roncero López. Madrid: Castalia.

Hooper-Greenhill, Eilean. 1992. *Museums and the Shaping of Knowledge*. London and New York: Routledge.

– 2000. *Museums and the Interpretation of Visual Culture*. London and New York: Routledge.

Hopkins, John H. 2017. *The Genesis of Roman Architecture*. New Haven, CT: Yale University Press.

Huergo, Humberto. 2006. "El zurrón de Polifemo: Naturaleza y alegoría en el *Polifemo* de Góngora." *Bulletin of Spanish Studies*, no. 83: 187–212. doi:10.1080/1475382062000346162.

Hui, Andrew. 2016. *The Poetics of Ruins in Renaissance Literature*. New York: Fordham University Press.

Insdorf, Annette. 2017. *Cinematic Overtures: How to Read Opening Scenes*. New York: Columbia University Press.

Iversen, Erik. 1993. *The Myth of Egypt and Its Hieroglyphs in European Tradition*. Princeton, NJ: Princeton University Press.

Jardine, Lisa. 1996. *Worldly Goods: A New History of the Renaissance*. New York and London: Norton.

Jardine, Lisa, and Jerry Brotton. 2000. *Global Interests: Renaissance Art between East and West*. Ithaca, NY: Cornell University Press.

Jauralde Pou, Pablo. 1987. "'Miré los muros de la patria mía' y el *Heráclito cristiano*." *Edad de Oro* 6: 165–87. https://revistaseug.ugr.es.

– 1991. "Las silvas de Quevedo." In *La silva*, edited by Begoña López Bueno, 157–80. Seville: Publicaciones de la Universidad de Sevilla.

– 1999. *Francisco de Quevedo (1580–1645)*. Madrid: Castalia.

Johnson, Christopher, ed. and trans. 2009. *Selected Poetry of Francisco de Quevedo*. Chicago: University of Chicago Press.

Johnson, Geraldine A. 2020. "Embodying Devotion: Multisensory Encounters with Donatello's *Crucifix* in S. Croce." *Renaissance Quarterly* 73, no. 4: 1179–1234.

Jones, Ann Rosalind, and Peter Stallybrass. 2000. *Renaissance Clothing and the Materials of Memory*. Cambridge: Cambridge University Press.

Juan de la Cruz, San. 2002. *Cántico espiritual y poesía completa*. Edited by Paola Elia and María Jesús Mancho. Barcelona: Crítica.

Juárez Almendros, Encarnación. 2006. *El cuerpo vestido y la construcción de la identidad en las narrativas autobiográficas del Siglo de Oro*. London: Tamesis.

Kallendorf, Hilaire, ed. and trans. 2011. *Francisco de Quevedo: Silvas*. Lima: Universidad Nacional Mayor de San Marcos.

Kallendorf, Hilaire, and Craig Kallendorf. 2000. "Conversations with the Dead: Quevedo and Statius, Annotation and Imitation." *Journal of the Warburg and Courtauld Institutes* 63: 131–68.

Karmon, David. 2011. *The Ruin of the Eternal City: Antiquity and Preservation in Renaissance Rome*. Oxford: Oxford University Press.

King, Willard F. 1960. "The Academies and Seventeenth-Century Spanish Literature." *PMLA* 75, no. 4: 367–76. https://www.jstor.org.

– 1963. *Prosa novelística y academias literarias en el siglo XVII*. Madrid: Imprenta Silverio Aguirre Torre.

Klein, Lisa M. 1997. "Your Humble Handmade: Elizabethan Gifts of Needlework." *Renaissance Quarterly* 50, no. 2: 439–93.

Kleiner, Fred S. 1991. "The Trophy on the Bridge and the Roman Triumph over Nature." *L'Antiquité Classique* 60, no. 1: 182–92. https://www.jstor.org.

Klibansky, Raymond, Erwin Panofsky, and Fritz Saxl. 1964. *Saturn and Melancholy: Studies in the History of Natural Philosophy, Religion and Art*. New York: Basic Books.

Koos, Marianne. 2014. "Wandering Things: Agency and Embodiment in Late Sixteenth-Century English Miniature Portraits." *Art History* 37, no. 5: 836–59.

Kristeva, Julia. 1989. *Black Sun: Depression and Melancholia*. Translated by Leon S. Roudiez. New York: Columbia University Press.

Kritzman, Lawrence D. 1991. *The Rhetoric of Sexuality and the Literature of the French Renaissance*. Cambridge: Cambridge University Press.

Lacan, Jacques. 1977. "The Function and Field of Speech and Language in Psychoanalysis." In *Écrits: A Selection*, translated by Alan Sheridan, 30–113. New York: Norton.

Laguna, Ana María G. 2009. *Cervantes and the Pictorial Imagination: A Study on the Power of Images and the Images of Power in Works by Cervantes*. Lewisburg, PA: Bucknell University Press.

Lara Garrido, José. 1980. "Notas sobre la poética de las ruinas en el barroco." *Analecta Malacitana* 3, no. 2: 385–99.

– 1999. "El motivo de las ruinas en la poesía del siglo de oro, funciones de un paradigma nacional: Sagunto." In *Relieves poéticos del siglo de oro: De los textos al contexto*, 251–308. Málaga: Analecta Malacitana.

Las Casas, Bartolomé de. 1965. *Historia de las Indias*. 3 vols. Edited by Agustín Millares Carlo. Mexico: Fondo de Cultura Económica.

Lazure, Guy. 2018. "Fashioning Fame: Fernando de Herrera's Anotaciones as a Space of Knowledge." In "Poesía y Materialidad," edited by Albert Lloret and Miguel Martínez. Special issue, *Calíope: Journal of the Society for Renaissance and Baroque Hispanic Poetry* 23, no. 2: 69–92.

Lefebvre, Henri. (1974) 1991. *The Production of Space*. Translated by Donald Nicholson-Smith. Oxford: Blackwell.

Lewis, Flora. 1997. "The Wound in Christ's Side and the Instruments of the Passion: Gendered Experience and Response." In *Women and the Book: Assessing the Visual Evidence*, edited by Lesley Smith and Jane H.M. Taylor, 204–29. London: British Library; Toronto: University of Toronto Press.

Lleó Cañal, Vicente. 1979. *Nueva Roma: Mitología y humanismo en el renacimiento sevillano*. Sevilla: Diputación Provincial de Sevilla.

– 1999. "Los techos pintados de la Casa de Pilatos." In *Velázquez y Sevilla: Estudios y Catálogo*, 2:173–81. Sevilla: Junta de Andalucía.

Lloret, Albert, and Miguel Martínez, eds. 2018. "Poesía y materialidad." Special issue, *Calíope: Journal of the Society for Renaissance and Baroque Hispanic Poetry* 23, no. 2.

López Bueno, Begoña. 1990. *Templada Lira: 5 estudios sobre poesía del siglo de oro*. Granada: Editorial Don Quijote.

López Grigera, Luisa. 1975. "La silva 'El pincel' de Quevedo." In *Homenaje al Instituto de Filología y Literaturas Hispánicas "Doctor Amado Alonso" en su Cincuentenario, 1923–1973*, 221–42. Buenos Aires: Losada.

– 1987. "Análisis de un soneto de Quevedo." *Cuardernos de Filología Hispánica*, 7, 105–16. https://dialnet.unirioja.es.

López Torrijos, Rosa. 1985. *La mitología en la pintura española del Siglo de Oro*. Madrid: Cátedra.

– 1999. "El techo de la casa del poeta Juan de Arguijo." In *Velázquez y Sevilla: Estudios y Catálogo*, 2:183–96. Seville: Junta de Andalucía.

Lucan. 1993. *Pharsalia*. Translated by Jane Wilson Joyce. Ithaca, NY: Cornell University Press.

Macaulay, Rose. 1967. *The Pleasure of Ruins*. New York: Walker & Co.

Mackenney, Richard S. 2002. "'A Plot Discover'd?' Myth, Legend and the Spanish Conspiracy against Venice in 1618." In *Venice Reconsidered: The History and Civilization of an Italian City-State, 1297–1797*, edited by John Jeffries Martin and Dennis Romano. 185–216. Baltimore, MD: Johns Hopkins University Press.

Maravall, José Antonio. 1979. *Poder, honor y élites en el siglo XVII*. Madrid: Siglo Veintiuno de España.

Martinengo, Alessandro. 1982. "La 'Vida de Quevedo' de Paolo Tarsia." In *Homenaje a Quevedo*, edited by Victor García de la Concha, 59–68. Salamanca: Universidad de Salamanca.

Mauss, Marcel. 1990. *The Gift: The Form and Reason for Exchange in Archaic Societies*. Translated by W.D. Halls. New York: Norton.

McGann, Jerome J. 1991. *The Textual Condition*. Princeton, NJ: Princeton University Press.

McKenzie, D.F. (1986) 1999. *Bibliography and the Sociology of Texts*. Cambridge: Cambridge University Press.

Micó, José María. 2001. *El "Polifemo" de Góngora: Ensayo de crítica e historia literaria*. Barcelona: Ediciones Península.

Milhou, Alain. 1983. *Colón y su mentalidad mesiánica en el ambiente franciscanista español*. Valladolid: Seminario Americanista de la Universidad de Valladolid.

Mitchell, W.J.T. 1994. "Word, Image, and Object: Wall Labels for Robert Morris." In *Picture Theory: Essays on Verbal and Visual Representation*, 241–79. Chicago: University of Chicago Press.

– ed. (1994) 2002. *Landscape and Power*. 2nd edition. Chicago: University of Chicago Press.

Morán, J. Miguel, and Fernando Checa. 1985. *El coleccionismo en España: De la cámara de maravillas a la galería de pinturas*. Madrid: Cátedra.

Moreno Castillo, Enrique E. 2004. "Anotaciones a la silva 'Roma Antigua y moderna' de Francisco de Quevedo." *La Perinola*, no. 8: 501–43. https://hdl.handle.net/10171/5622.

Mulvey, Laura. 1989. *Visual and Other Pleasures*. Bloomington: Indiana University Press.

Necipoğlu, Gülru. 1989. "Süleyman the Magnificent and the Representation of Power in the Context of Ottoman-Hapsburg-Papal Rivalry." *The Art Bulletin* 71, no. 3: 401–27. https://link.springer.com.

Nora, Pierre. 1995. "Between Memory and History: *Les Lieux de mémoire*." Translated by Marc Roudebush. In *Histories: French Constructions of the Past*, edited by Jacques Revel and Lynn A. Hunt, 631–43. New York: New Press.

Orozco Díaz, Emilio. (1947) 1989. "Ruinas y jardines: Su significación y valor en la temática del Barroco." In *Temas del Barroco: De poesía y pintura*, 121–76. Granada: Universidad de Granada.

Őstenberg, Ida. 2009. *Staging the World: Spoils, Captives, and Representations in the Roman Triumphal Procession*. Oxford: Oxford University Press.

Ovid. 1969. *The Art of Love and Other Poems*. Edited by G.P. Goold. Translated by J.H. Mozley. Cambridge, MA: Harvard University Press.

– 1984. *Metamorphoses*. 2nd ed. Edited and translated by Frank Justus Miller. Revised by G.P. Goold. 2 vols. Cambridge, MA: Harvard University Press.

– 1996. *Tristia. Ex Ponto*. 2nd ed. Translated by Arthur Leslie Wheeler. Revised by G.P. Goold. Cambridge, MA: Harvard University Press.

Pacheco, Francisco. 1956. *Arte de la pintura*. Edited by F.J. Sánchez Cantón. 2 vols. Madrid: Instituto de Valencia de Don Juan.

Pade, Marianne, ed. 2011. *On Renaissance Academies*. Proceedings of the International Conference "From the Roman Academy to the Danish Academy," 11–13 October 2006. Rome: Edizioni Quasar.

Pando-Canteli, María J. 2016. "Letters, Books, and Relics: Material and Spiritual Networks in the Life of Luisa de Carvajal y Mendoza (1564–1614)."

In *Devout Laywomen in the Early Modern World*, edited by Alison Weber, 294–311. Abingdon, Oxon: Routledge.

Panofsky, Edwin. 1967. "The Neoplatonic Movement and Michelangelo." In *Studies in Iconology*, 171–230. New York: Harper & Row.

Parker, Alexander A. 1977. *"Polyphemus and Galatea": A Study in the Interpretation of a Baroque Poem*. Austin: University of Texas Press.

Paster, Gail Kern. 2004. *Humoring the Body: Emotions and the Shakespearean Stage*. Chicago: University of Chicago Press.

Paz, Octavio. 1982. *Sor Juana Inés de la Cruz o Las trampas de la fe*. Barcelona: Seix Barralt.

Petrucci, Armando. 1998. *Writing the Dead: Death and Writing Strategies in the Western Tradition*. Translated by Michael Sullivan. Stanford, CA: Stanford University Press.

Pinillos Iglesias, María de las Nieves. 2001. *Hilando oro: Vida de Luisa de Carvajal*. Madrid: Laberinto.

Plato. 1993. *Philebus*. Translated by Dorothea Frede. Indianapolis, IN: Hacket.

Poggi, Giovanni, Paola Barocchi, and Renzo Ristori, eds. 1965–83. *Il carteggio di Michelangelo*. 5 vols. Florence: Sansoni.

Ponce Cárdenas, Jesús, ed. 2010. *Fábula de Polifemo y Galatea*. Madrid: Cátedra.

Propertius. *Elegies*. 2006. Edited and translated by G.P. Goold. Cambridge, MA: Harvard University Press.

Quevedo, Francisco de. 1648. *El parnasso español, monte en dos cumbres dividido, con las nueve musas castellanas*. Edited by Joseph Antonio González de Salas. Madrid: Diego Díaz de la Carrera.

Quintana, Gerónimo de. (1629) 1980. *A la muy antigua, noble y coronada Villa de Madrid: Historia de su antigüedad, nobleza y grandeza*. Facsimile edition. Madrid: Ábaco.

Quintero, Maria Cristina. 2000. "'Con ansia estrema de mirar': Another Look at the Gaze in Spanish Golden Age Poetry." *Revista de Estudios Hispánicos* 34, no. 3: 489–513. https://www.academia.edu.

– 2016. "The Space of Empire and the Place of Patronage in Some Panegyric Sonnets by Luis de Góngora y Argote." *Calíope: Journal of the Society for Renaissance and Baroque Hispanic Poetry* 21, no. 2: 5–18. https://muse.jhu.edu.

Redworth, Glyn. 2008. *The She-Apostle: The Extraordinary Life and Death of Luisa de Carvajal*. Oxford: Oxford University Press.

– ed. 2012. *The Letters of Luisa de Carvajal y Mendoza*. Translated by David McGrath and Glyn Redworth. 2 vols. London: Pickering & Chatto.

Regosin, Richard L. 1995. "Montaigne and His Readers." In *A New History of French Literature*, edited by Denis Hollier, 248–53. Cambridge, MA: Harvard University Press.

Rey, Alfonso. 1997. "Vida retirada y reflexión sobre la muerte en ocho sonetos de Quevedo." *La Perinola*, no. 1: 190–211. https://studylib.es.

Rhodes, Elizabeth. 1998. "Luisa de Carvajal's Counter-Reformation Journey to Selfhood (1566–1614)." *Renaissance Quarterly* 51, no. 3: 887–911. doi:10.2307/2901749.

– 2000. *This Tight Embrace: Luisa de Carvajal y Mendoza (1566–1614)*. Milwaukee, WI: Marquette University Press.

Richardson, Catherine. 2011. *Shakespeare and Material Culture*. Oxford: Oxford University Press.

Rivers, Elias L. 1966. *Renaissance and Baroque Poetry of Spain, with English Prose Translations*. New York: Dell.

Robertson, Clare. 2015. *Rome 1600: The City and the Visual Arts under Clement VIII*. New Haven, CT: Yale University Press.

Rocha de Sigler, María del Carmen, ed. 1994. *Francisco de Quevedo: Cinco silvas*. Salamanca: Ediciones Universidad de Salamanca.

Roth, Michael S., Claire L. Lyons, and Charles Merewether. 1997. *Irresistible Decay: Ruins Reclaimed*. Los Angeles: Getty Research Institute for the History of Art and the Humanities.

Ruiz Sánchez, Marcos. 1999. "Las ruinas deshabitadas: Notas sobre la tradición elegíaca del tema de las ruinas en la poesía neo-latina." *Excerpta Philologica: Revista de Filología Griega y Latina de la Universidad de Cádiz*, no. 9: 349–76. https://dialnet.unirioja.es.

Rutledge, Steven H. 2012. *Ancient Rome as a Museum: Power, Identity, and the Culture of Collecting*. Oxford: Oxford University Press.

Sáez, Adrián J. 2015. *El ingenio del arte: La pintura en la poesía de Quevedo*. Madrid: Visor.

Salinas, Pedro. (1966) 1980. *Reality and the Poet in Spanish Poetry*. Translated by Edith Fishtine Helman. Westport, CT: Greenwood Press.

Sánchez, José. 1961. *Academias literarias del Siglo de Oro español*. Madrid: Gredos.

Sánchez Cantón, F.J., ed. 1956–9. *Inventarios reales: Bienes muebles que pertenecieron a Felipe II*. 2 vols (X.1, XI.2). Madrid: Real Academia de la Historia.

Sánchez Jiménez, Antonio, and Adrián J. Sáez, eds. 2018. *Siete memoriales españoles en defensa del arte de la pintura*. Madrid and Frankfurt: Iberoamericana/Vervuert.

Saslow, James W. 1986. *Ganymede in the Renaissance: Homosexuality in Art and Society*. New Haven, CT: Yale University Press.

Sauer, Carl Ortwin. (1925) 1967. "The Morphology of Landscape." In *Land and Life: A Selection from the Writings of Carl Ortwin Sauer*, edited by John Leighly, 315–50. Berkeley and Los Angeles: University of California Press.

Saxl, F. 1957. *Lectures*. 2 vols. London: Warburg Institute.

Schiesari, Juliana. 1992. *The Gendering of Melancholia: Feminism, Psychoanalysis, and the Symbolics of Loss in Renaissance Literature.* Ithaca, NY: Cornell University Press.

Schroth, Sarah. 2008. "A New Style of Grandeur: Politics and Patronage at the Court of Philip III." In *El Greco to Velázquez*, ed. Schroth and Baer, 77–121.

Schroth, Sarah, and Ronni Baer, eds. 2008. *El Greco to Velázquez: Art during the Reign of Philip III.* Boston: Museum of Fine Arts.

Schulz, Juergen. 1968. *Venetian Painted Ceilings of the Renaissance.* Berkeley: University of California Press.

Schwartz, Lia. 1995. "Ficino en Quevedo: pervivencia del neoplatonismo en la poesía del siglo XVII." *Voz y letra* 6, no. 1: 113–35.

Seneca. (1917–25) 2014. *Epistles.* Translated by Richard M. Gummere. 3 vols. Cambridge, MA: Cambridge University Press.

Serrera, Juan Miguel. 1996. "Velázquez and Sevillian Painting of His Time." In *Velázquez in Sevilla: National Gallery of Scotland*, edited by David Davies, Enriqueta Harris, and Michael Clark, 37–43. Edinburgh: Trustees of the National Galleries of Scotland.

Shephard, Tim. 2010. "Constructing Identities in a Music Manuscript: The Medici Codex as a Gift." *Renaissance Quarterly* 63, no. 1: 84–127. https://sheffield.academia.edu.

Sherman, Daniel J., and Irit Rogoff, eds. 1994. *Museum Culture: Histories, Discourses, Spectacles.* Minneapolis: University of Minnesota Press.

Silver, Larry. 2008. *Marketing Maximilian: The Visual Ideology of a Holy Roman Emperor.* Princeton, NJ: Princeton University Press.

Simmel, Georg. 1959. "The Ruin." In *Georg Simmel, 1858–1918: A Collection of Essays*, edited by Kurt H. Wolff and translated by David Kettler, 259–66. Columbus: Ohio State University Press.

Skyrme, Raymond. 1982a. "'Buscas en Roma a Roma': Quevedo, Vitalis, and Janus Pannonius." *Bibliothèque d'Humanisme et Renaissace* 44, no. 2: 363–7. https://www.academia.edu.

– 1982b. "Quevedo, Du Bellay, and Janus Vitalis." *Comparative Literature Studies* 19, no. 3: 281–95. https://cafedelasciudades.com.ar.

Slater, John. 2008. "From *Historia Naturalis* to Historia au naturale: Lastanosa and the Naked Truth." In *The Gentleman, the Virtuoso, the Inquirer: Vincencio Juan de Lastanosa and the Art of Collecting in Early Modern Spain*, edited by Mar Rey-Bueno and Miguel López-Pérez, 30–46. Newcastle, UK: Cambridge Scholars.

Smith, Paul Julian. 1989. "The *Polifemo*: Narrative and Catachresis." In *The Body Hispanic: Gender and Sexuality in Spanish and Spanish American Literature*, 60–7. Oxford: Clarendon.

Soufas, Teresa Scott. 1990. *Melancholy and the Secular Mind in Spanish Golden Age Literature.* Columbia: University of Missouri Press.

Stinger, Charles L. 1998. *The Renaissance in Rome*. Bloomington: Indiana University Press.

Stratton, Suzanne L. 1988. "Spanish Miniatures of the 16th ad 17th Centuries." In *The Spanish Golden Age in Miniature: Portraits from the Rosenbach Museum & Library*, 15–30. New York: Spanish Institute.

Suida, William E. 1949. *A Catalogue of Paintings in the John & Mable Ringling Museum of Art*. Sarasota, FL: John & Mable Ringling Museum of Art.

"Symposium: The Aesthetics of Ruin and Absence." 2014. Special issue, *Journal of Aesthetics and Art Criticism* 72, no. 4: 429–49.

Tarsia, Pablo Antonio de. (1663) 1988. *Vida de don Francisco de Quevedo y Villegas*. Facsímil de la edición príncipe, Madrid, 1663. Edited by Melquíades Prieto Santiago. Aranjuez: Ara Iovis.

Ter Horst, Robert. 2013. "Francisco de Quevedo and the Poetic Matter of Patronage." In *Objects of Culture in the Literature of Imperial Spain*, edited by Mary E. Barnard and Frederick A. de Armas, 181–202. Toronto: University of Toronto Press.

Torres, Isabel. 2006. *The Polyphemus Complex: Rereading the Baroque Mythological Fable*. Special monograph issue, *Bulletin of Hispanic Studies* 83, no. 2.

– 2007. "Galatea … Rereading Góngora's *Polifemo* Stanzas 13–23." In *Rewriting Classical Mythology in the Hispanic Baroque*, edited by Isabel Torres, 55–70. Woodbridge, UK: Tamesis.

– 2013. *Love Poetry in the Spanish Golden Age: Eros, Eris, and Empire*. Woodbridge, UK: Tamesis.

Tovar Martín, Virginia. 1988. "La entrada triunfal en Madrid de Doña Margarita de Austria (24 de octubre de 1599)." *Archivo Español de Arte* 61, no. 244: 385–403.

Tuan, Yi-Fu. 1977. *Space and Place: The Perspective of Experience*. Minneapolis: University of Minnesota Press.

Valdivieso, Enrique, and Juan Miguel Serrera. 1979. *Catálogo de las pinturas del Palacio Arzobispal de Sevilla*. Sevilla: Sever-Cuesta.

Vasallo Toranzo, Luis, and Sergio Pérez Martín. 2013. "Francisco Giralte y el sepulcro del obispo Gutierre de Carvajal." *Archivo Español de Arte* 86, no. 344: 275–89.

Vasari, Giorgio. 1996. *Lives of the Painters, Sculptors and Architects*. Translated by Gaston du C. de Vere. 2 vols. New York: Knopf.

Vickers, Nancy. 1982. "Diana Described: Scattered Woman and Scattered Rhyme." In *Writing and Sexual Difference*, edited by Elizabeth Abel, 95–110. Chicago: University of Chicago Press.

Vilanova, Antonio. 1957. *Las fuentes y temas del Polifemo de Góngora*. 2 vols. Madrid: CSIC.

Villamediana, Conde de. 1969. *Obras*. Edited by Juan Manuel Rozas. Madrid; Castalia.

Villanueva, Darío. 2007. *La poética de la lectura en Quevedo*. Madrid: Ediciones Siruela.

Vincent, Robert Hudson. 2018. "Baroque Optics and Luis de Góngora's *Polifemo*." *MLN* 133, no. 2: 224–41.

Virgil. 1999, 2000. *Eclogues, Georgics, Aeneid, the Minor Poems*. Edited and translated by H. Rushton Fairclough. 2 vols. Cambridge, MA: Harvard University Press.

Vranich, Stanko B., ed. 1985. *Obra completa de Don Juan de Arguijo (1567–1622)*. Valencia: Albatros.

Wagschal, Steven. 2007. *The Literature of Jealousy in the Age of Cervantes*. Columbia: University of Missouri Press.

Wardropper, Bruce W. 1969. "The Poetry of Ruins in the Golden Age." *Revista Hispánica Moderna* 35, no. 4: 295–305. https://www.jstor.org.

Warwick, Genevieve. 1997. "Gift Exchange and Art Collecting: Padre Sebastiano Resta's Drawing Albums." *Art Bulletin* 79, no. 4: 630–46.

Weiss, Roberto. 1969. *The Renaissance Discovery of Classical Antiquity*. Oxford: Oxford University Press.

Welles, Marcia L. 1986. *Arachne's Tapestry: The Transformation of Myth in Seventeenth-Century Spain*. San Antonio, TX: Trinity University Press.

Wethey, Harold E. 1971. *The Paintings of Titian*. Vol 2. London: Phaidon.

Williams, Patrick. 2006. *The Great Favourite: The Duke of Lerma and the Court and Government of Philip III of Spain, 1598–1621*. Manchester, UK: Manchester University Press.

Wittkower, Rudolf. 1977. *Allegory and the Migration of Symbols*. Boulder, CO: Westview Press.

Wittkower, Rudolf, and Margot Wittkower. 1963. *Born under Saturn: The Character and Conduct of Artists; A Documented History from Antiquity to the French Revolution*. London: Weidenfeld & Nicolson.

Woods, M.J. 1978. *The Poet and the Natural World in the Age of Góngora*. Oxford: Oxford University Press.

Woods-Marsden, Joanna. 1998. *Renaissance Self-Portraiture: The Visual Construction of Identity and the Social Status of the Artist*. New Haven, CT: Yale University Press.

Wright, Elizabeth R. 2001. *Pilgrimage to Patronage: Lope de Vega and the Court of Philip III, 1598–1621*. Lewisburg, PA: Bucknell University Press.

Yates, Frances A. (1964) 1977. *Giordano Bruno and the Hermetic Tradition*. Chicago: University of Chicago Press.

Yermolenko, Galina I. 2010. *Roxolana in European Literature, History, and Culture*. Burlington, VT: Ashgate.

Zamora, Margarita. 1993. *Reading Columbus*. Berkeley: University of California Press.

Index

Toronto Iberic

1 Anthony J. Cascardi, *Cervantes, Literature, and the Discourse of Politics*
2 Jessica A. Boon, *The Mystical Science of the Soul: Medieval Cognition in Bernardino de Laredo's Recollection Method*
3 Susan Byrne, *Law and History in Cervantes' "Don Quixote"*
4 Mary E. Barnard and Frederick A. de Armas, eds., *Objects of Culture in the Literature of Imperial Spain*
5 Nil Santiáñez, *Topographies of Fascism: Habitus, Space, and Writing in Twentieth-Century Spain*
6 Nelson Orringer, *Lorca in Tune with Falla: Literary and Musical Interludes*
7 Ana M. Gómez-Bravo, *Textual Agency: Writing Culture and Social Networks in Fifteenth-Century Spain*
8 Javier Irigoyen-García, *The Spanish Arcadia: Sheep Herding, Pastoral Discourse, and Ethnicity in Early Modern Spain*
9 Stephanie Sieburth, *Survival Songs: Conchita Piquer's "Coplas" and Franco's Regime of Terror*
10 Christine Arkinstall, *Spanish Female Writers and the Freethinking Press, 1879–1926*
11 Margaret Boyle, *Unruly Women: Performance, Penitence, and Punishment in Early Modern Spain*
12 Evelina Gužauskytė, *Christopher Columbus's Naming in the* diarios *of the Four Voyages (1492–1504): A Discourse of Negotiation*

13 Mary E. Barnard, *Garcilaso de la Vega and the Material Culture of Renaissance Europe*
14 William Viestenz, *By the Grace of God: Francoist Spain and the Sacred Roots of Political Imagination*
15 Michael Scham, *Lector Ludens: The Representation of Games and Play in Cervantes*
16 Stephen Rupp, *Heroic Forms: Cervantes and the Literature of War*
17 Enrique Fernandez, *Anxieties of Interiority and Dissection in Early Modern Spain*
18 Susan Byrne, *Ficino in Spain*
19 Patricia M. Keller, *Ghostly Landscapes: Film, Photography, and the Aesthetics of Haunting in Contemporary Spanish Culture*
20 Carolyn A. Nadeau, *Food Matters: Alonso Quijano's Diet and the Discourse of Food in Early Modern Spain*
21 Cristian Berco, *From Body to Community: Venereal Disease and Society in Baroque Spain*
22 Elizabeth R. Wright, *The Epic of Juan Latino: Dilemmas of Race and Religion in Renaissance Spain*
23 Ryan D. Giles, *Inscribed Power: Amulets and Magic in Early Spanish Literature*
24 Jorge Pérez, *Confessional Cinema: Religion, Film, and Modernity in Spain's Development Years, 1960–1975*
25 Joan Ramon Resina, *Josep Pla: Seeing the World in the Form of Articles*
26 Javier Irigoyen-García, *"Moors Dressed as Moors": Clothing, Social Distinction, and Ethnicity in Early Modern Iberia*
27 Jean Dangler, *Edging toward Iberia*
28 Ryan D. Giles and Steven Wagschal, eds., *Beyond Sight: Engaging the Senses in Iberian Literatures and Cultures, 1200–1750*
29 Silvia Bermúdez, *Rocking the Boat: Migration and Race in Contemporary Spanish Music*
30 Hilaire Kallendorf, *Ambiguous Antidotes: Virtue as Vaccine for Vice in Early Modern Spain*
31 Leslie Harkema, *Spanish Modernism and the Poetics of Youth: From Miguel de Unamuno to* La Joven Literatura
32 Benjamin Fraser, *Cognitive Disability Aesthetics: Visual Culture, Disability Representations, and the (In)Visibility of Cognitive Difference*
33 Robert Patrick Newcomb, *Iberianism and Crisis: Spain and Portugal at the Turn of the Twentieth Century*
34 Sara J. Brenneis, *Spaniards in Mauthausen: Representations of a Nazi Concentration Camp, 1940–2015*
35 Silvia Bermúdez and Roberta Johnson, eds., *A New History of Iberian Feminisms*

36 Steven Wagschal, *Minding Animals in the Old and New Worlds: A Cognitive Historical Analysis*
37 Heather Bamford, *Cultures of the Fragment: Uses of the Iberian Manuscript, 1100–1600*
38 Enrique García Santo-Tomás, ed., *Science on Stage in Early Modern Spain*
39 Marina Brownlee (ed.), *Cervantes' "Persiles" and the Travails of Romance*
40 Sarah Thomas, *Inhabiting the In-Between: Childhood and Cinema in Spain's Long Transition*
41 David A. Wacks, *Medieval Iberian Crusade Fiction and the Mediterranean World*
42 Rosilie Hernández, *Immaculate Conceptions: The Power of the Religious Imagination in Early Modern Spain*
43 Mary Coffey and Margot Versteeg, eds., *Imagined Truths: Realism in Modern Spanish Literature and Culturex*
44 Diana Aramburu, *Resisting Invisibility: Detecting the Female Body in Spanish Crime Fiction*
45 Samuel Amago and Matthew J. Marr, eds., *Consequential Art: Comics Culture in Contemporary Spain*
46 Richard P. Kinkade, *Dawn of a Dynasty: The Life and Times of Infante Manuel of Castile*
47 Jill Robbins, *Poetry and Crisis: Cultural Politics and Citizenship in the Wake of the Madrid Bombings*
48 Ana María Laguna and John Beusterien, eds., *Goodbye Eros: Recasting Forms and Norms of Love in the Age of Cervantes*
49 Sara J. Brenneis and Gina Herrmann, eds., *Spain, World War II, and the Holocaust: History and Representation*
50 Francisco Fernández de Alba, *Sex, Drugs, and Fashion in 1970s Madrid*
51 Daniel Aguirre-Oteiza, *This Ghostly Poetry: Reading Spanish Republican Exiles between Literary History and Poetic Memory*
52 Lara Anderson, *Control and Resistance: Food Discourse in Franco Spain*
53 Faith Harden, *Arms and Letters: Military Life Writing in Early Modern Spain*
54 Erin Alice Cowling, Tania de Miguel Magro, Mina García Jordán, and Glenda Y. Nieto-Cuebas, eds., *Social Justice in Spanish Golden Age Theatre*
55 Paul Michael Johnson, *Affective Geographies: Cervantes, Emotion, and the Literary Mediterranean*
56 Justin Crumbaugh and Nil Santiáñez, eds., *Spanish Fascist Writing: An Anthology*
57 Margaret E. Boyle and Sarah E. Owens, eds., *Health and Healing in the Early Modern Iberian World: A Gendered Perspective*

58 Leticia Álvarez-Recio, ed., *Iberian Chivalric Romance: Translations and Cultural Transmission in Early Modern England*
59 Henry Berlin, *Alone Together: Poetics of the Passions in Late Medieval Iberia*
60 Adrian Shubert, *The Sword of Luchana: Baldomero Espartero and the Making of Modern Spain, 1793–1879*
61 Jorge Pérez, *Fashioning Spanish Cinema: Costume, Identity, and Stardom*
62 Enriqueta Zafra, *Lazarillo de Tormes: A Graphic Novel*
63 Erin Alice Cowling, *Chocolate: How a New World Commodity Conquered Spanish Literature*
64 Mary E. Barnard, *A Poetry of Things: The Material Lyric in Habsburg Spain*